A Romantic Look at Early Canadian Furniture

Heritage

A Romantic Look at Early Canadian Furniture

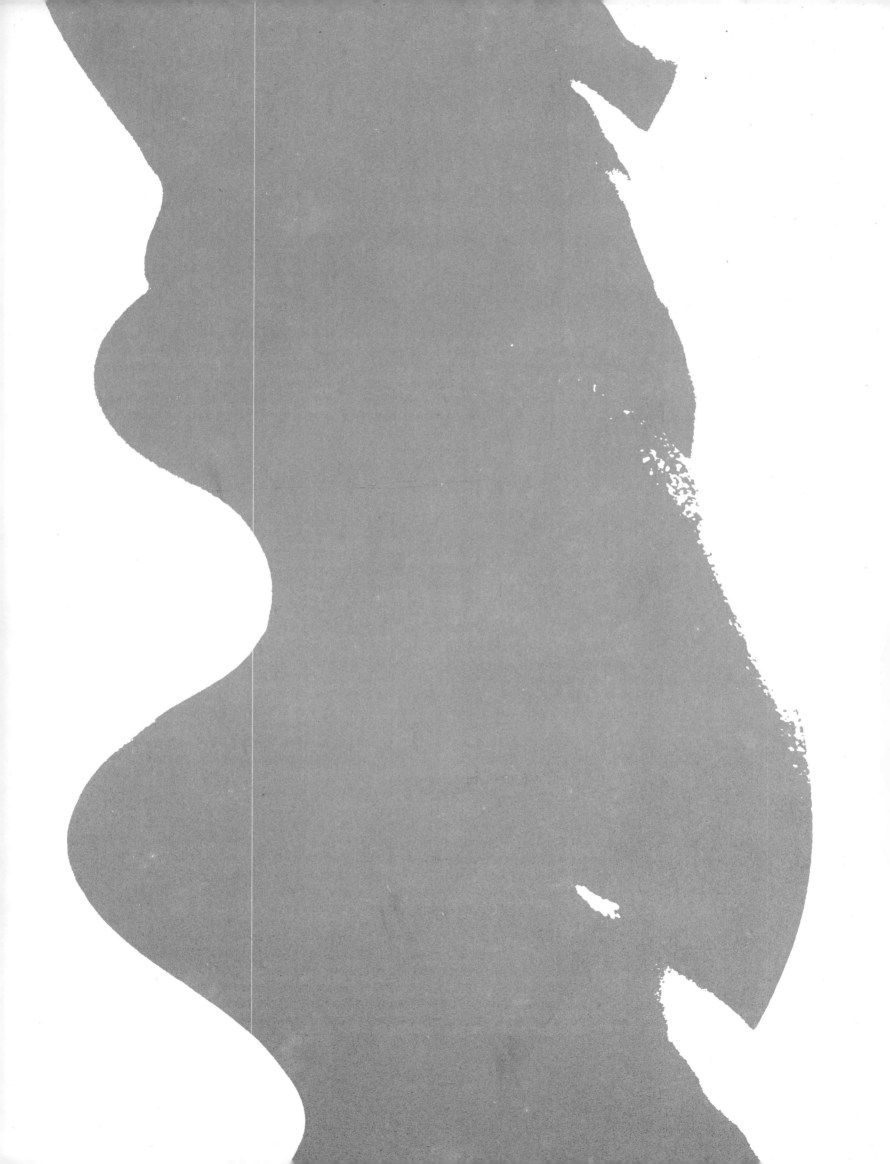

A Romantic Look at Early Canadian Furniture

Heritage

Scott Symons/Photographs by John de Visser

McClelland and Stewart Limited

Toronto/Montreal

This book is in Celebration of a people, culture, history, and faith...It is for you.

0-7710-8377-7

The Canadian Publishers
McClelland and Stewart Limited
25 Hollinger Road, Toronto 374

Printed and bound in Italy

Contents

Preface

It is a pleasure to write some words at the beginning of this splendid book, splendid both in what is said about the furniture by Mr. Symons and in how it is photographed by Mr. de Visser. Symons shows us consummately that the furniture of any time or place cannot be understood as a set of objects, but rather as things touched, seen, used, loved, in short, simply lived with through the myriad events which are the lives of individuals, of families, of communities, of peoples. For an object is any thing (whether stone or tree or even human being) when it is held by another outside himself so that it can be organised to show its potentialities for being at the disposal of other wills, as an undifferentiated source of supply.

As our society has become objectified, we can either buy furniture in Simpsons-Sears, or distantly look at it in museums. There is a long choice of supplies for us to buy: Italianate or Swedish, Louis Quinze or Chippendale, in teak or oak or plastic, depending on our bank accounts and our fantasies. As bank accounts are always quantitive, whether in Dallas or Dusseldorf, in Twickenham or Toronto, so our fantasies move to become homogeneous. Furniture becomes the fixtures, whether in Holiday Inns or apartments. The question remains whether the heart's core can be sustained by things supplied in the same way as motor cars under the principle of organised obsolescence. Museums are needed in an age of quick change and therefore of quick destruction. This therapy has been produced by the same conditions which have produced what it would cure. Museums are not places where we can live with things. (Many of the pieces Symons describes are now in museums, but he obviously much prefers to find them elsewhere.)

Symons is telling us of furniture before it was so objectified; the furniture of three distinct societies which came together into Canada. He knows that furniture among these people was not a supply of objects, but things brought forth in the arts of those who shared a communality of existence with others who would live amidst it. He shows this about things as different as a fireplace in Halifax, a cupboard in Ontario or a communion table of a French Canadian bishop. He knows therefore that the modern distinctions between 'fine' art and 'craft' and between 'art' and 'technique', are not adequate to understand these things, because their makers assumed that beauty was not something divided from daily utility, and that 'art' was in its origins the Latin translation of 'techné'.

The writing in this book brings the furniture before us because Symons is gifted with what I can only describe platitudinously as 'the educated imagination'. In our imaginative judgements we bring together the particular perceptions of our sensibilities with the universal entities. Leaving aside the hiddenness of what it would be to make Mozart's Quintet in G Minor, when we listen to its particular melodies and harmonies we may partake in a statement of what always and everywhere is. Though in listening we never leave those particular melodies and harmonies, they draw us out to the enjoyment of what can never be completely actualised in them. Symons' enjoyment of this furniture (and his help to our enjoyment) arises from the way his sensibility never loses its hold on the particular pieces before us. Yet he is led out and out from those particularities to the people who made them and lived with them, to the community they inhabited, and beyond that to the differing riches of the European civilisation which lay unbroken behind them in all its surging richness of politics and religion and art. What is so satisfactory about Symons' descriptions is that he never uses the furniture as an excuse for a pedantic lecture, but rather by making us look at the furniture leads us out into the complexities of lived traditions. The man of intellect without sensibility does not bother to look at furniture; the man of sensibility without intellect cannot know fully what is given to him in his looking. In the 'educated imagination' of this book we can be helped both to look and to know.

Furniture is tied closely not only to the love of the good, but to the love of our own, which may be only slightly good. It is more our own even than our clothes because it is liable to be longer lasting as jewelry or china. Of all things it is only less our own than our bodies and the bodies of those we love. 'Las Meninas' is also a thing, but it attains to such universality of statement that who could dare to say that they possess it, except a king as representing a people. Perhaps a Spaniard could understand it in more detail than anybody else because of his particular awareness of what Velasquez made there; but its very universality of statement opens it to the understanding of man qua man. We can possess furniture as our own because of its very limitation. But in understanding it we need particularly an intimate knowledge of the detailed lives of those who live with it as their own. This kind of knowledge is best available to those who are of the same own. In his book Symons shows forth the knowledge of what it was to be a Canadian in the eighteenth and nineteenth centuries. To be such was precarious and even ambiguous—something so dividedly poised as that part of North America which had not broken its connection with western Europe. It was, however, something unique. Symons knows that uniqueness in its details, because he knows his fate is to be that and he has loved it. Perhaps that fate can be escaped by some who desire to be cosmopolitan and who love to be part of more powerful or fuller cultures. However, escaping a particular fate may not result in transcending it; one may enter something so general as to be almost nothingness, and therefore unsustaining. From knowledge and love of his limited fate as Canadian, Symons brings to his study of furniture an appreciation of the blood and bones of Canadian history, from which one can learn and learn. He apprehends its concrete immediacy in a way quite absent in the liberal and positivist textbooks from which our children are asked to learn about their past. If one wishes to know what was unique, ambiguous and precarious about Canada, one should read his jokes and gaieties with attention.

In writing of Canadian furniture Symons does not forget how different were the cultures of Ontario, Québec and the Maritimes; nor does he forget the differences in each, for example between Nova Scotia and New Brunswick. Ontario loyalism is Symons' own, in a way that the Maritimes or Québec are not. But it is evidence of the fact that we did in some sense come together that he can open himself to the other cultures as his own. This appears in his understanding of how greatly different were the styles of Nova Scotia and New Brunswick from those of Ontario, and how in some ways that of New Brunswick was nearer to Ontario than that of Nova Scotia. It appears even more strongly in his unequivocal recognition that the furniture of Québec shows itself as more finely beautiful than the others. He has an openness to the attainments of French North America which no citizen of the United States has yet shown. For example, it is singularly lacking in the barren comments of so rare an American artist as Henry James. What a different history Canada might have had, if more Ontario loyalists and even some Methodists had so apprehended the reality of Québec. Indeed his admiration of what Québec has been appears even more deeply in his proclamation of the sadly necessary yet impossible choice; were it inevitable that he must be either a French Canadian or part of the imperial republic, he would choose the former.

George Grant
May, 1971

Introduction

Furniture is faith!

It is one of our forms of believing, or of not believing. One of the modes of our knowing, or of willing to not know. It is an intimate and revelatory part of our culture, showing us the shape and shapes of that culture. Furniture tells us how we view—in a given time and place—our very body and being.

If we know what our furniture is, then we know who we are, in the profoundest sense—and we cannot escape with a counterfeit identity. Documents, newspapers, books, men's words—these may lie. But furniture does not lie. It presents to our naked eye, we ourselves—if we dare but see.

Canadian furniture, of course, like most furniture of the Western World, grows bodily from the Cathedrals of the Middle Ages. The Church, Christendom, gave birth to our Western civilization. And the apogee of the Church, in the Middle Ages, was the Cathedral— the Seat, or Chair, of the Bishop, and the House of God. Within this House—including the presbytery beside— could be found, in the twelfth, thirteenth, and fourteenth centuries, the basic furniture we know today: chairs (thrones), benches, stools, desks and reading-stands, tables (altars), cupboards, even beds. Some of this furniture was crude, some sumptuous. For example, I wonder if any chairs ever made have equalled some of the choirstalls carved in this medieval period. These stalls are in effect singing-chairs—chairs made to sing and worship from. And they have served their purpose now for nigh a thousand years!

Of course furniture, much fine furniture, was made long before the Medieval Church. As early as the third millenium Before Christ, simple, and sometimes sumptuous, furniture could be found in Egypt and other parts of the Middle East, as well as in China. I can well remember the start of amazement and wonder I felt when I saw pictures of furniture made for the mother of Kheops, Queen Hetep-heres, around 2500 B.C. It was burial furniture, gold-sheathed, and of incredible simplicity and magnificence. I could only

think of the solid silver furniture made for Louis XIV over 4000 (!) years later, at Versailles, equally as opulent, and to my taste considerably less attractive. The Queen's furniture seemed something one could actually live with—or, in her case, die with. Whereas the silver furniture of Louis XIV seems for show.

And anyone who spends a few moments looking at Greek vases, the red or black ware of the sixth and fifth centuries Before Christ, will quickly know that Greek furniture and decor was as fine, as elegant, and as lucidly and palpably reasonable as marble statues by Praxiteles, or dialectics by Socrates.

So, too, Roman villas were often sumptuous. And fine Roman furnishings found their way as far as Great Britain nearly 2000 years ago.

But just as our Western civilization in essence grows from the Medieval Church, so does much of our furniture. And insofar as we recognize this fact, we can recognize what French and English Canadian furniture tells us about the nature of Canadian culture, will, and faith.

Let us briefly look at the Cathedrals. Largely built between 1100 A.D. and 1500 A.D., these Medieval super-Churches are, each of them, a whole world in stone. When you see one on the horizon, such as Chartres, you sense a summation, a centre, the focal point of an entire culture and community. When you approach one, you see the face of an entire world— carved in stone: angels, animals, queens, peasants, burghers and kings, on the frontal. When you enter such a building, you are engulfed in an entire reality which somehow reflects the reality of nature and the outer world you have just left. And when you enter a side chapel from the nave of the Cathedral body as such, you enter into a world within the world of the Cathedral. You are in fact experiencing the pre-Copernican reality of Western civilization. A reality of worlds-within-worlds-within-worlds (without end!). And our phrase that so-and-so "is in seventh Heaven" —meaning that she or he is very happy—comes from the pre-Copernican cosmology, of which Medieval Cathedrals are excellent visual and palpable evidence.

When you enter a European Cathedral you literally penetrate a common, a communal, experience. You have the sensation of everything imbedded, everything substantial, everything in touch with everything else. The date and the place of the Cathedral really doesn't matter: France, Spain, Italy, England, or Germany; Romanesque, Venetian Gothic, Perpendicular English—the experience is one and the same, variations on a theme. And if you permit yourself to be swept up in the Cathedral, instead of simply looking *at* the building as some subject fit for instant-Kodachrome; if you mesh with the Cathedral (which *is* the invitation it proffers), then you are truly *in* some visual correlative to the Medieval Christian theology of the True Cross, the Real Presence of Christ in Communion, and Mary Queen of the World. You understand—on the spot—such central beliefs of early Christendom. They are *not* superstitions, but strong, simple expressions of what you, feeling, know. To pun pertinently, within the body of such buildings, "seeing *is* believing"! And the post-Renaissance world of three-dimensions and of systematized doubt disappears.

These huge Churches were not only miniatures of the universe, not only microcosms. They were also macrocosms. They were pieces of furniture, blown to huge size. This is not as far-fetched as it seems. As Emile Mâle has pointed out, European Cathedrals derive in important measure from small Middle Eastern and Eastern ivory carvings. The Cathedrals are miniature ivories blown large. And this is precisely the feeling one often has with Medieval Cathedrals . . . the feeling of something miniature made cosmic.

And within these churches, the actual furnishings, episcopal chair, table for sacrifice (the High Altar), and the Monstrance for the Host, or the reliquaries for Holy relics . . . these in themselves are often miniature cathedrals, just as the Cathedral can feel like a magnified Altar table or like an Episcopal Seat—which is precisely what a cathedral is.

Everything is a part of everything else. Everything *is* everything else. Everything is not only universal, but its own universe. It is in this way that, for a medieval peasant, everthing in a Cathedral *is*, somehow (inexplicably but inexorably), a piece of the True Cross. The bench, the Bible lectern, the kneeling-desk (prie-dieu)—everything is either a piece of Christ's Body or . . . it is nothing. Worse, it is sin and death— some kind of spiritual cancer! Said simply: within the world of the Cathedrals, everything is either Celebration of God's word—or it is a Mortal Sin. Everthing is either Alleluia or anguish.

Now the point I want to make here is simple, but fundamental. In the medieval world of Cathedraldom, we see the matrix of furniture as we know it today. Yet in such a medieval world there is no such thing as "furniture"—that is, no such thing as "mere furniture." There is really no such thing as an isolated object performing an independent, separated function. Everything is doing everything, visually speaking. Everything is *being* everything. You don't really see the High Altar as a table, nor the Episcopal Seat as a chair separate from the church. To use a modern term, everything "comes together." The usual intellectual term for such a world is "organic." But for the citizens of the European Medieval world, to describe something as "organic" would be absurd. For such Europeans, objects, people, places, reality, had never been "apart." The very idea of "severance" was, to them, repugnant, and replete with disaster.

Most Canadians will sense themselves in some way "At Home" in a European Cathedral. For many there is simply a feeling of spiritual arrival or peace, as well as some recognition of "having been there before." This may seem strange, because the Medieval Cathedral is an experience which is largely denied to us in North America. There is nothing quite like the great European Cathedrals here. A few fragments at most. Anglican fragments, as in Saint John's, Newfoundland, or the Butterfield Ecclesiological Gothic of the Cathedral in Fredericton. Or something like the monumental experience of the Episcopal Cathedral in Washington—at once transcendental... and bland. Or else Catholic presences, such as the Church of Notre Dame, in Place d'Armes, Montréal.

No—the presence of the Cathedral experience is more subtle, and indirect, in our Canadian living. It can be found pervading French Canadian parish churches... despite their small size and apparent Baroque interiors. And it can be found in a number of important secular nineteenth century buildings, such as the Parliament Buildings in Ottawa—especially the East and West Blocks and the Library there. Or in University College and Victoria College, in Toronto. Even in the Ontario (or British Columbian) Parliament Buildings.

Buildings such as these combine to suggest to us some powerful direct and indirect medieval roots within Canadianism.

But it is even closer to home that we find the basic evidence—staring us in the face. Not in the few actual Medieval survivals in our culture, nor in the monumental Medieval revival buildings, but in our grandmother's, or great-grandmother's, Victorian parlour! Enter a nineteenth century Ontario, or French Canadian, or Maritime home, one which has any of its original furnishings intact—and two times out of three your experience is a "churchy" one... one of frills and lace and "frescoes" (the ornated wallpapers), and chairs which look gothicky. . . . It is, somehow, the feeling of a side-chapel in some European Medieval Cathedral. Or—said somewhat negatively (but not meant negatively)—it has the air of a friendly funeral parlour!

Most old Canadian families—and almost all new Canadian families—have such a "pocket cathedral" ancestral home behind them. Here, or in Europe.

If we find the sources of Canadian furnishings—both spiritual and domestic—in the Middle Ages, it is with the Renaissance that we get the beginnings of a long

slow "severance," or detachment—both spiritual and domestic.

The simplest example of this is in art—with the creation (the re-creation) of three-dimensional perspective. Medieval painting and art—like Medieval architecture—swarms all round you. But Renaissance painting finally gives you detached figures, places, objects. The historical lineage of this is easily traced— the line from Giotto through Piero della Francesca, Botticelli, to Raphael. Before Giotto, painted figures are still immersed in their surroundings. Giotto, as it were, begins to "detach" them.

It is at this time, that Medieval furniture starts to become the furniture we know today—detached, movable objects. That is, it is at the time of the Renaissance, in Europe, that the object as an object is born. The object which is no longer some organic portion of a wonder-full, heaven-and-hellish life-scape; but simply an independent, functional, secular object. Something merely to be used, as against something with which we participate in living, celebrating, or mourning. In short, the object ceases to be part of our flesh and our faith—and becomes our tool.

It can be said that in the Middle Ages there were no "objects"—everything was a "subject." Everything was part of us as we were part of everything. Everything partook of the Body of God, incorporated here, on earth, in Christ's Church. But as the effects of the Renaissance took hold of Europe, everything ceased—in the long run—to be a "subject," and became simply detached "object."

But there is a period in the middle, which we could genuinely label "the Moment of Truth," when Medieval mysticism and Renaissance mind-fullness are wed. Arbitrarily, say 1475 to 1525, in the high arts of Rome and Florence. That period when Leonardo and Raphael and Michelangelo endow us with the greatest paintings of Western civilization since the Caves of Lascaux. And what is common to all of these paintings is firstly some total engulfing "heady" (hallucinating) Medieval presence—a presence we could term "Real Presence," in artistic correlation to the Christian doctrine. And secondly the full-born object: the detailed, defined, detached-yet-still-attached object.

This magnificent moment, when subject and object are each a part of some single Being—each defined, yet married, unified—this plenitudinous moment is superbly summarized in Raphael's painting of the Disputa. This painting is a triumphant and lucid application of the rules of three-dimensional perspective. It uses this new perspective, not merely to define individuals, but as it were to open people and objects more fully to us; unlike later three-dimensional paintings, which seem to close down and merely isolate people and objects. And thus it retains the "heady" Medieval presence.

In essence, both the style of Raphael's picture, and its subject, the papal affirmation of the Real Presence of Christ in Holy Eucharist, are one and the same thing: the statement that the world IS one...is "organic," and not a world of detached "discrete particulars." Raphael's painting does for our eye and our spirit what the Catholic doctrine of the Real Presence does for our soul: it harmonizes body, mind, and spirit. It harmonizes Heaven and earth.

And it is not accidental that a large copy of Raphael's Disputa is to be found over the entry to the Sacred Heart Chapel of Notre Dame Church, in Place d'Armes, Montréal.

This Moment of Truth is a short and hazardous one in Europe. Erasmus, on the European mainland embodies it. In England, Thomas More does.

Soon after 1525, the story of the Western world becomes one of fragmentation. Almost of deliberate fragmentation. The mind and the body—the eye and the object—these do not stay together, but are divorced. The Dream of Christendom is shattered.

We have the Reformation versus the Counter-Reformation. Some long-term division becomes the very nature of Western civilization. Some kind of schizophrenia en bloc. And—to use traditional language—the word is no longer made flesh, nor the flesh made word. And this is the importance and the tacit point of McLuhan's Gutenburg Galaxy: the invention of print occurs within roughly half a century of Raphael's Disputa. That is, at the very moment when the Head of Christendom, the Pope, affirms the unity of experience, the invention of print has begun to dispute this unity. And the Western World formally enters our era, in which progress and reality are merely seen as the gradual incarnation of reason.

What in effect happens, in European experience, is that mind and spirit declare open formal war on each other! The Protestant world moves progressively towards a reality of mere-mind. And the Catholic world defensively moves towards a reality of sheer mysticism. The Protestant world makes intellectual moves which culminate in Utilitarianism, arithmetic democracy, and material comfort: life as a consolation prize. While Catholicism takes refuge in an architecture of hallucination: the Baroque.

It is at the time of this "Great Divide," between mere-mind and sheer-mysticism, that modern England and France are born. France remaining Catholic (as Henri IV said, "Paris was worth a Mass"!)—and England moving half-way forward to Protestantism, and half-way back to an earlier, simpler Catholicism—in the Anglican Church.

This difference in choice, between the French Cartesian Catholicism on the one hand, and the less rationalized and rather more pedestrian Anglicanism, is reflected not only in the difference between the precise high French genius of Corneille and Racine and the more turbulent earthy genius of Shakespeare, but also in French and English furniture. The difference, finally, between the sumptuous "churchy" furnishings of the Court at Versailles—with its high High Style (out-Poping St. Peter's in pomp), and the Cavalier, and then Whig bourgeois, furnishings of Restoration and Orange England. Quite simply there is at once more "mind," *and* more mass and Mass, in French furniture of the seventeenth century. Whereas in English furniture one senses less of each of mind and mass—some half presence of each—a physical correlative to what a Catholic would sense as the Half-Real Presence in Anglican Holy Communion. And, in passing, be it noted, it is this Half-Presence of each of mind and matter, with some slight added disjunction, which—two centuries later, in 1850—creates the distinctive Ontario farm home!

By the middle of the seventeenth century, the Great Divide between mind and matter and between mind and spirit has formalized, and the virtually official architecture of the Catholic Counter-Reformation is the Baroque. To me, the Baroque is quite simply a case of "mass-in-motion": mass, substance, is picked up—in the flesh—and borne bodily Heavenwards. It is a case of the emotions (and of the will!) making off with mere-mind. The culmination of this sleight-of-flesh is the great Baldaquin by Bernini, in St. Peter's, Rome. Designed in 1642, this 100-foot-high whorl of marble and majesty "blows your mind."

And this is when French Canadiana is born—truly "under a Baldaquin"!—in affirmation of millenial Medieval Catholicism, as part of the Catholic Counter-Reformation.

This is also the period when English-American furniture is born, a product of Puritan Dissent against overblown Medieval Catholicism—and affirming the Reformation. And it is from within the culture of English-American furniture that English Canadiana is born—in special circumstances.

In short—French Canadiana is a case of the Medieval world trying to include the Renaissance mind, but defending itself against mere-mind. French Canadiana is a case of the Catholic Baroque.

And, in contrast, English Canadiana is a case of the Enlightenment, but not quite: because English Canada retains some thread of its Medieval roots, finally rejects the revolutions of the Age of Reason and superimposes elements of the Medieval revival of mid-Victorianism. Which is definitive.

The Case of Canadiana

The tie between France and la Nouvelle France, from 1604 to 1759, is direct and effectively feudal. Thus it should be easy to follow the evidences of French styles as adapted in French Canada. And if French Canada is "born under Bernini's Baroque baldaquin"—artistically and spiritually speaking then the essential qualities of French Canadian furniture should be joy, majesty, glory—a fundamental experience of celebration. And there will also be some constant element of "trompe-l'oeil"; some constant spoliation of mere three-dimensional perspective in aid of transcendence. Or, more precisely, some constant use of three-dimensional perspective *within* a sense of mass which transcends the mere box of three-dimensional perspective.

In short, French Canadiana, in its profounded being, will reveal itself as a eucharistic experience. A furniture of celebration. And each piece of furniture will have some tincture of a Cathedral to it . . . some touch of the experience you receive, at best, in a Medieval Cathedral. In the true poetic sense, French Canadiana will be a piece of "the True Cross." Which is exactly how it was conceived!

The *particular* form this furniture takes will be the defining form of French Canadianness. It will be the Real French Canadian Identity . . . the underlying and eternal one.

Let the evidence—the furniture—speak for itself, in our naked eye.

* * *

The English Canadian case is more complex, in its component parts—but finally as straight forward.

Firstly, English Canadian furniture styles do not derive uniquely from England. The basic English Canadiana style is *American*...via the Loyalists. Thus there is a dual material source for English Canadiana—England, *and* the English colonies in America from 1607 to 1776.

Secondly, while Protestant and Anglican England are born in partial dissent from continental European Catholicism, and while English America (the Thirteen Colonies) are born in further dissent from England's demi-Dissent—English Canada is largely born during the American Revolution, in recoil from American Dissent. In a nutshell, English Canada is born in dissent from dissent at dissent (English Canada is a powerful and positive complex of apparent negatives!). Thus there is a dual religious and political root to English Canada: a further push towards the Protestantism of Progress, which is English North America. And a recoil back to some original English, catholic, millenial sources. This is the swing against American Puritan extremism.

Given this duality, let us examine in more detail each of the English and American traditions behind English Canadiana. Firstly, a hidden sensibility syllogism in English furniture styles—from 1550 to 1870; a sensibility sequence which has to do with the fact that the story of Western society, and in particular Protestant society, from the Renaissance on is that of a schizophrenic battle between mind and flesh, and also between mind and Grace, or spirituality.

In the Elizabethan era in England, we see the transition from Medieval to Mannerist—say 1550 to 1620. It is a literal case of the "flesh made word." Whole châteaux used to spell, architecturally, a single letter. Prior to Elizabeth's reign, you have a Latin Church whose truth is expressed liturgically, in ritual—embodied—performance. After Elizabeth's reign, and with the King James Version of the Bible, you have an English Church whose truth is expressed both in embodied liturgy and in the native tongue: a Church both of the flesh and of the word. The marriage, finally, is

Laudian. The result is, in effect, a Protestant's Catholicism.

In the Jacobean and Cromwellian period—from 1603 to the Restoration of the Crown in 1660—the world as flesh (physical or metaphysical) is under great strain. It is under mental attack—just as, symbolically, the concept of the Real Presence in Communion is under corrosive attack. Thus we get the poetry of Dean John Donne—at once straining to sustain final credulity and undergoing an agony of doubt.

In North America New England is born from the English Puritan element of this era. Whereas the Virginia Settlement, be it remembered, remains Cavalier—an important distinction for Loyalist Canada.

The Stuart Restoration of 1660 is literally a "restoration of the flesh"—both carnally and ecclesiastically. The Puritanism of Cromwell's Ironsides (the phrase is telling...and echoes through to Victorian Ontario Grit politics and architecture!)—the Puritanism of Cromwell is rejected, and England under Charles the Second is truly ejaculaTory. Furniture is ebullient once again! But a process has set in which is clear. The flesh—and Real Presence—may have been restored, but it is on the wane. Examine the change in English poetry from Donne to Dryden. All Donne's torment of metaphysical flesh dies down. And we are left with a smoothed-out rhyming line in couplets. Culminating in Pope's *Rape of the Lock*—the Englishman is being housebroken.

Equally symbolic in this period is the burning of the Tudor Medieval Palace, Nonsuch—and the rebuilding of Saint Paul's Cathedral as an exercise in reason.

This slowly subsiding flesh of Englishness can be followed under William-and-Mary (1688-1702) and the Whig Revolution. A revolution against the Anglo-Catholicism of James II, and a further move towards parliamentarianism.

Under Queen Anne (1702-14) English furniture undergoes a startling change in form and feel. It is suddenly suave, svelte, curvaceous. The tea table takes on social and visual importance. The reign of Good Queen Anne is a "Copernican Revolution," socially and stylistically. What has happened is not only some continued subsiding of the tumescent flesh of Elizabethan and Stuart days, and not only the rise of some rational line of reason—but also (just *look* at Queen Anne furniture) a precise change in gender of furniture! Stuart furniture is full of flair and frill—but it is, finally, a male object. It is, precisely, phallic! The object, in Stuart days, has both a religious and a sexual correlative: it reflects both Real Presence in religion, and phallic presence in the flesh. The Object, in the Stuart era, *is* Holirood. But under Queen Anne, furniture (perhaps understandably, certainly agreeably) becomes female!

The Georgian era in England, broadly speaking 1714 to 1837, sees the full rise of Parliament and England's Age of Reasonableness. The Age when that virago of sheer Reason, Voltaire, can praise English political and social institutions. In the Georgian period all flesh *is* progressively made into words. The very word "Parliament" itself comes from the French "parler"—to speak. And Parliament is the palace where words are king! And the written word the law!

This is not merely a metaphoric description of the Georgian period. Regard Georgian furniture. Furniture which by self-definition is fleshly (it is, after all, made to carry or service the human body!)—even furniture is no longer a thing primarily of the hands, the fingertips—but is now derived from Design Books. Furniture becomes mind-maps made flesh; made flesh?—no, made wood! Because while seventeenth century English furniture feels flesh, feels embodied, Georgian furniture increasingly feels wooden, albeit ornately wooden.

The Georgian era witnesses the triumph of mind over matter. The term "Enlightenment" is exact: everything in furniture loses substance.

In the Victorian era in England, again broadly speaking 1837 to 1939 (in Canada, till 1967), we have the triumph of bourgeois utilitarian sentimentality (what Wilde described as "cynicism on a bank holiday"). And an interesting thing occurs: the Enlightenment thickens up: it receives the "body" of the rising middle class. Furniture, which in the late eighteenth century had essentially become visual essays in applied Reason (e.g., the introduction to Sheraton's *Director*, with its dissertation on geometry!)—furniture thus frozen in the mind's eye now takes on weight and heft again. You could say that Methodism is added to Whig Anglicanism, and becomes Victorian Britishness. But the flesh somehow never quite breaks through alive. The result is Victorian rococo—which looks like cast iron!

The sensibility sequence in English furniture—and life—from 1550 to 1939, then, is clear enough—it is one from the Word made Flesh, to flesh made words!

To this add the basic American tradition.

Firstly, there is New England puritanism, which is embodied precisely in New England furniture—or rather "disembodied" precisely. Because the fundamental quality of this furniture is one of leanness, attenuation, lack of mass and carving and decoration. The New England Windsor chair form is the clinical puritan verity! And, of course, the religious correlative to New England furniture becomes Unitarianism—than which nothing could be further from the bi-millenial European tradition of Real Presence in Church or in daily living. Or, said architecturally—New England is characterized by clapboard façades, flat planes of wood—and what becomes a geometric exercise in reason. I am thinking obviously of New England Federal houses (say 1790-1825), but this tendency to "disembodiment" is there from the time of the Mayflower, and remains today!

In contrast to New England Puritantics is the seventeenth and eighteenth century tradition of Philadelphia, Baltimore, and the Southern gentry. I think here, for example, of the splendorous rococo

Philadelphia Highboys (amongst the great furniture achievements of any age!) Or the mid-eighteenth century chinoiserie panelling of Gunston Hall, in Virginia. Or the substantial and substantive intellectual presence of Jefferson's Monticello.

Of course, in this American South, there is a strong tradition of Episcopalianism (American Anglicanism)—as against New England's Puritanism. Americans simply conveniently forget how many of the leaders in the American Revolution worshipped in Christ Church, Philadelphia, and belonged to the squirearchy.

Thus, in the early American Colonies, there are two major cultural traditions—Puritan New England and Cavalier South. In the American Revolution, and finally in the American Civil War, the Puritanism wins—ruthlessly! and America becomes the United States—Greater New England.

Thus, in the United States, as in England, the tradition which dominates is the one which turns spirit and flesh into words! The one which turns substance into mind.

All of this may sound beside the point, either to furniture in general or to Canadiana in particular. It isn't! What we witness in this brief story of Anglo-American culture and design (and religion) is the birth of the mere-mind at the expense of every other element of reality! The birth of utilitarian rationality and the correlative decline of body, substance, flesh, sheer animal intuition, and—in religion—Real Presence. In short, the rise of reason and the decline in capacity for joy.

And this decline (call it the Quiet Devolution!)—this decline in feelings, sensibility, sentience, and carnal presence, coincides with two other facts: Firstly, the imperceptible loss of the "male object," which ends up smothered (smother-lovered) in gynarchical Victorian parlour decor. And, secondly, the formal split of mind from body, and the slow death of the body as such—resulting in what is now clearly a con-

commitant hypertrophy of mind and of will! In short, through furniture and decor in the English-speaking world we can follow the growth of modern alienation over a period of four centuries. The evidence of what Norman Mailer names "the Plague" is disconcerting and implacable.

The importance of this Quiet Devolution for Canadians and Canadiana is this. French Canadiana is NOT born in this context...or not entirely. French Canadiana remains Medievally Baroque. It remains "together," if partially mindless.

But English Canada and English Canadiana *are* most definitely born within this psychic civil war of mind versus embodied spirit. And if we define how and what we shall have defined English Canadian civilization in some important measure.

Firstly, the American tradition behind English Canada. It is the conservative element which comes North after the American Revolution. It is the American Tory, or Cavalier, tradition which comes to Canada as Loyalists. Not necessarily the wealthy or educated (though some of these—especially in the Maritimes)—but more often the conservative folk. These Loyalists *are* what George Grant terms them: Lockeans, with a dash of Anglicanism. These, plus the Calvinist conservative puritans, as against the Antinomian radicals who remain to buy and build Greater New England.

And these Loyalists, both in their religion and beliefs, as in their furniture, architecture and manners, combine more substance and more decor that is also decorum, than the Yankees. Which is legitimate and logical, if you feel about it.

Secondly, the English and British tradition, coming into English Canada. This is the element from the historic English compromise—between Catholicism as a faith and Protestantism as a mode of progress. Call it some kind of Cavalier Protestantism. The early (sixteenth and seventeenth century) West Country

men settling in Newfoundland. The King's men—
soldiers and their families in the eighteenth century...
in the Maritimes and Quebec. Plus Jacobitic and
jaundiced Scots. And in the nineteenth century, folk
Irish (wildly Catholic—and wildly protesting). Plus
that important influx of solid stolid English yeomen
and gentlemen, who run so much of Victorian
Canada. And all culminating in that medieval Gothic
revival that is the English Canadian Victorian
farmhouse....

The combined result of this English and British culture,
plus the American Loyalist one, is Confederation,
and that quality which underlies so much of English
Canadiana: a kind of stolid substantiality which is at
once decorous (but not very decorated). A desire to
conserve yet move ahead, be "with it" in style. Some
combination of High style and hick folk. A stated
desire to preserve elements of a thousand year old
heritage from Christendom, and an equal desire to
stand solid on one's own two feet.

Call it...Barnyard Whig!—with a Cavalier nostalgia
that *is* more real than mere nostalgia. The result is
that hard-headed English-Canadian Romanticism
which is constantly disclaiming itself, and talking
about being tough and realistic, and then winks at
you with half a smile, and some hopes. Or did....

Thus, French Canadiana: a hallucinogenic furniture
of Being and of Celebrations.

And English Canadiana: a stolid furniture of enduring
and of becoming, with kinetic vestiges of Being and
of Eucharist!

This is the stage: now for the Players!

Scott Symons

A Romantic Look at Early Canadian Furniture

. . . entering University College—
Victorian bastion . . . and inside
the hall, this great carved golden-oak
newel post, Grand Dragon of the
Honest Ontario Yeoman-made-good.
Carved for the rebuilding of
University College, Toronto, 1890-2.

Newfoundland Sidechair

The room with its reticulating maple chest-of-drawers (yeoman, all gussied up an no place to go), and the plangent four-posted bed, each commandeering my eye

(out the window the gulls, wheeling—understudy albatrosses—so much lighter than air in the presence of these ponderosities)

my eye is glimpsed neither by the gulls nor the mid-Victorian respectability, but over in the corner, perched, light as the gulls yet freighted with the substance of both chest and bed, with an added elegance

(like Whistler's Mommy, dressed up to court!)

my eye moving from bowed back and centred sunburst, down the (oh) trim prim spoked waist to those slightly tapered legs in front, slightly withdrawn at the back, as I turn to acknowledge this unexpected grace seducing me, and

even as I turn I realize that this High-born Lady has feet of clay

because once my eyes touch the ground and flow back up, what impresses me is no High Bric-a-brac Style, but rather the solidity, some warm embodiment. Which, I note, is the simple squared seat—that's it! This is an invitation to sit, whereas so often High-and-Lordly Style is a thinly veiled invitation to remain standing

oh yes, first the well-mannered eye is caught and reassured that here is quality. And then, almost

immediately, the flesh of the eye is also caught . . . one is no longer held at arm's length

come, kerthump, and dump cares in the lap and

as I sit I realize that this is truly Newfoundland, Sir Humphrey Gilbert's New-Found-Land, nearly four hundred years ago, when Spenser was awriting the *Faerie Queen* and Nicholas Hilliard drawing miniature dandies fought against the Armada

West Countrie men, fishing the sea, cajoling the tough land . . . and building cosy homes like the Mallard House, early eighteenth century and still a home, at Quidi Vidi, pronounced Kitty Vitty. . . .

this chair, this fusion of medieval joint stool, really, with its wooden-pegged simplicity as well as Adamesque sun-burst and echoes of Hepplewhite

this culture spans four centuries, halfway between New England folk astringency and Old Country stolidity, truly mid-Atlantic. . . .

outside, the gulls have come to rest, on a rock clustered. It is I who float, in this chair. . . .

Wood: maple and pine
Date: about 1840
Place: Canadiana Gallery, Royal Ontario Museum.

Windsor Chair

For a long time I've been aware of a curious relationship between English Metaphysical poetry and the American Windsor chair. I could not see how, but my sensibility simply told me that they were cousins. I left it at that.

But I began studying the chair more closely—dozens of examples, scattered over half a continent—and as I did I realized that this style was a world-embracing witticism: bulbs, turns, spindles, the saddled seat, the whole chair whorling, encircling, clenching and releasing, delineating and defining—this chair is some microcosm of the Seven Heavenly Spheres, held together in interlacing and interbracing joinery.

Then, browsing one day, I read what T. S. Eliot wrote of the Metaphysical poet Marvell—

"It is more than a technical accomplishment, or the vocabulary or syntax of an epoch; it is what we have designated tentatively as wit, a tough reasonableness beneath the slight lyric grace."

And I knew that this definition of style was a precise one, too, of the Windsor chair; in my mind the link was now clear.

Later, in the work of two New England poets of the late seventeenth and early eighteenth centuries, I saw a fact: in Anne Bradstreet and Edward Taylor

the English line of poetic wit had crossed the Atlantic. Passing through Puritanism, it came out, sometime in the mid eighteenth century, not as lyric poetry, but as the lean, strong, functional poetry that is also the American Windsor chair. Case concluded: this style of chair, a unique form, *is* a product of the same mind and culture that produced Donne and Herbert and Marvell.

But the American Windsor is more than just a functional by-product of the line of wit! Siegfried Giedion said:

"The Windsor Chair is as outstandingly important in the history of American furniture as the balloon frame is in the history of American housing."

Yes. It is a precise conquest of space and need.

This chair first came to Canada in the Maritime Provinces and Newfoundland in the mid eighteenth century, moved with the Loyalists to Québec and Ontario by the end of that century. It is an intrinsic part of our Canadian culture.

Wood: ash and pine
Date:　about 1800
Label:　J. Humeston, Halifax
Place:　Nova Scotia Museum, Citadel Hill, Halifax

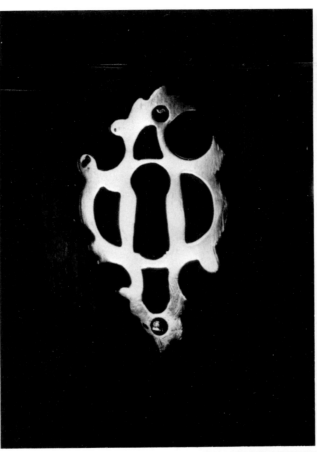

Flame Birch Corner Cupboard

Scott died seeking the Antarctic Pole, as much a witness to the Christian and the Gentleman and the loyal Public Servant as Sir Thomas More. Sir Edmund Hillary climbed Mount Everest and gave the feat to his Queen as Coronation. President Fox of Western University spent ten years questing for the Hart's Tongue Fern in Ontario's Bruce Peninsula—and, finding her, wrote a book as testimony and tribute. Even sempiternal Prime Minister Mackenzie King left a statue to Sir Galahad (and a youngman friend), now standing outside Canada's Parliament.

For ten years now I have known about this Corner Cupboard! Rumours of its presence floated through to Ontario: a Flame Birch Cupboard. No, not Tigerstripe, but rarer still, ENFLAMED—that rroaring wood, let loose—

> with bracket feet, Chippendale,
> and a deep cornice
> with Gothic dentation, and. . . .

It was like hearing of some strangest beautibeaste lurking in the deepest wilds, like Okapi, unseen. . . . Something come down to us live from the flickering lights of Lascaux: phantasmagoric, for real.

I wanted to see it. (Ah, coward, say it out! I LUSTED TO SEE IT!) At least a photo—but no one knew where, precisely. I forgot about it, till about five years ago. Then a friend mentioned it again . . . it had bowed fronts to the shelves, bodicurve matching the flames, I knew it had to be so!

And then one day I saw a photograph, black and white, no denying the presence, and I knew where the beast had its lair: Sackville, Middle Sackville, the Hendersons. . . .

And now it is 1970, August. After a week of unearthing the beauties of Thomas Nisbet, Craftsman, I am en route out of the Loyalist City, Saint John, en route along the South Shore of New Brunswick— those rumpling hills and white-towered churches, New England Meeting Houses with the Trinity added as tower, extra dimension! . . . en route with a rendezvous two hundred miles on in Middle Sackville. . . .

standing in the left-hand corner of the dining room. Ahh—

Tall. Taller than I had felt He was . . . and through the dim light of late afternoon, the ripe birch flames shimmering—like Apricot Brandy after your third glass as your lover leans forward, flush, flushed, and giving. . . .

Wood: curly birch
Date: about 1790
Place: Mr. & Mrs. J. W. Henderson,
          Middle Sackville, New Brunswick.

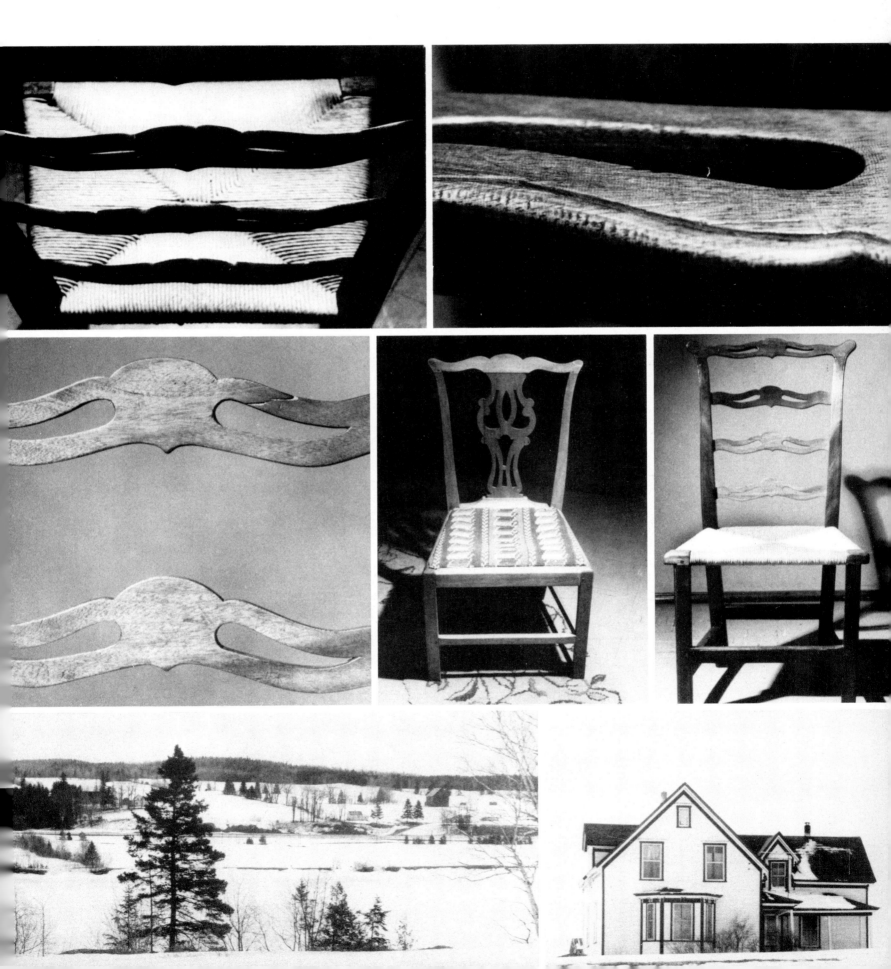

Chippendale Sidechairs

September of 1835, for the first time, in the columns of Joseph Howe's Halifax newspaper, *The Novascotian*, the "sayings and doings" of Sam Slick appeared, Sam Slick, the Yankee clockmaker, itinerant in Nova Scotia, said gent to be known within the decade on both sides of the Atlantic: a shrewd and original crackerbarrel philosopher. And through Sam's lips came the definitive assessment of the Yankee-American, as well as of that Yankee-Britisher who is the Nova Scotian.

Thomas Chandler Haliburton, member of a prominent Tory family which had migrated to Nova Scotia before the American Revolution, was Sam Slick's author. In his writings, Mr. Slick is paired with the conservative, traditionalist Squire Thomas Poker. Poker tones Slick down, puts him intelligently in his place—which is not high, culturally, seen in the light of, say, Socrates, Cicero, Sir Thomas More, or even Thomas Haliburton himself. And yet: Sam Slick gingers up Squire Poker and the conservative Nova Scotians who, by Yankee standards, are truly asleep.

And this is a considerable achievement, taking the best of two worlds, British, American; for a long time it was the unstated basis of English Canada's character.

These chairs, also, embody the achievement. The tops of them—the finished elegance of high Chippendale, English-rococo, design, without the equivalent English chair's encrusted carving. The bottoms—a much simpler form, with overlapping front T-bars and what would probably originally have been rush seats. That is, the top of each chair is Squire Poker; and the bottom is the Yankee, Sam Slick.

And *that*, gintlemen, is the Bluenoser!

Wood: mahogany
Date: about 1800
Place: Nova Scotia Museum, Citadel Hill, Halifax.

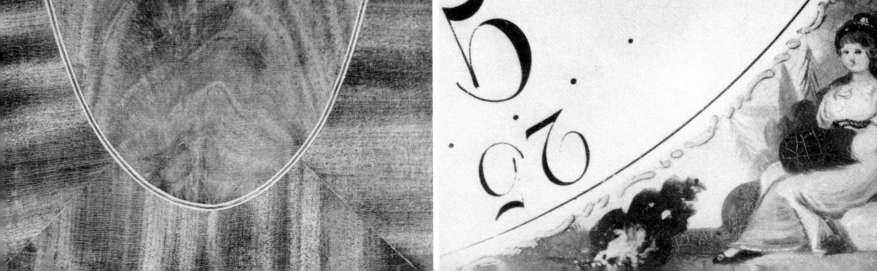

Tulles Grandfather Clock

 Bearing the label of Tulles, Palliser, and M'Donald, Halifax, this grandfather clock is an example of Maritime and English Canadian craftsmanship at its best. As a piece of furniture it may initially strike you as a massive uprising monument—strong and thick— culminating in that almost antlered head. And this massiveness *is* one of its qualities (it is, after all, scarcely a wrist watch!). But a second appraisal of this piece reveals an elegant, delicate, even shrewd work of sheer mental calculation. In fact, it is this presence of virtually carnal mass within a product of the mind which defines both the quality of this clock and the culture which produced it.

In 1800, and right on into living memory, culture, quality, physical creativity—these lived together in Canada. Meditation with the hands, and touch with the mind, were not separated in any significant way.

The Maritime culture of quality was once presided over by the Duke of Kent, father of Queen Victoria. He helped design such buildings as Halifax's Old Town Clock, and his own Garden Rotunda—both of which show that Halifax was as cosmopolitan as Jefferson's Monticello. So does this handsome clock. In fact work by Tulles and his partners was so fine that a Regency drumtop table with their label sold a few years ago, in London, as an English piece, and is now in Brazil. And English Regency furniture is the finest in the world.

This clock would be beautiful in any refined home,

or manor or château in the world. Its equine arched top is a baroque tradition of the late seventeenth century—a form which dies out of high furniture styles generally by 1750—except in American highboys, and in grandfather clocks. And it is this crowning head which helps to give the clock such a feeling of mass. But the rest of the design is essentially flat and geometric; not carved, not turned. There is the precise circle of the inlaid base, and the equally fine oval inlay of the waist, enclosed by careful veneering. These and the changing Moon on the clock face, with the dial for date, all reveal the presence of a detached and precise mind at work. These tell us that this clock is a work of the intellectual Enlightenment.

Add a final indicative detail: those squared pillars on the upper clock case. They belong both within the calculating mind of the Age of Reason, and the square (cubicular) culture of much Canadianism.

Thus this handsome and elegant clock is as much a part of the "religion" of the Enlightenment in Canada as Québec carved furniture is of the Faith of the Roman Catholic Baroque and Counter Reformation.

Woods: mahogany and satinwood
Date: about 1820
Label: Tulles, Palliser, and M'Donald, Halifax
Place: Nova Scotia Museum, Citadel Hill, Halifax

THOS. NISBET,
CABINET MAKER & UPHOLSTERER,
PRINCE WILLIAM STREET,
Saint John, New Brunswick;
WHERE MAY BE HAD,
MATTRASSES various kinds; Sophas and Sopha Beds; Chairs; Tables, Sideboards; Portable Beds and Writing Desks; Bed and Window Cornishes and Curtains; and every thing in the Cabinet and Upholsterer Line, made on moderate terms.
Old Furniture Repaired, or exchanged for New.

Nisbet Card Table

Driving into Saint John after visiting the Tilley Homestead in Gagetown, where Sir Leonard Tilley was born in 1816, New Brunswick Father of Confederation.... and musing on that fine, almost New England, clapboarding of the house, the filagree wood verandah fretwork....

Well, I've chosen the secondary routes where I could, today driving along the Saint John River washing this lovely roll of hills, a Horned Grebe at Pine Point, and that hand-built church... built by a man inspired by Elbert Hubbard's homilies—corny homilies, but they inspired a man to build this song to God that gave me peace....

"Saint John—The Loyalist City," the sign says.

I weave my way through to my target, the New Brunswick Museum, and ask for the Nisbet Table.??? No one knows. Or has even heard of it. It's not on display.

We search the storage rooms. Not there. I am stunned, numbed. Wander the Museum, desultory in dismay....

But over in a corner, by a basement door, is a centre of sweet calm, a balm in resonant red-browns... like a Wood Thrush rustling the Autumn ferns....

and I know instantly it can be only one, can only be....

such svelte flow of wood, coiling like a rising taper, and the sure curve of the corners and (glancing over my shoulder) I am over beside, touching....

yes, it is He alright....

and open the swivel top, yes, the Label: Thomas Nisbet Cabinet: Saint John.

What irony . . . a century and a half later, here in a small basement gallery of the museum meant to house you, holding the Visitors' Book for a psychedelic mod-art exhibit. Thomas Nisbet, the Duncan Phyfe of Canada.

Only one thing to do... pick you up and carry you, upstairs where you belong. Where people can see you and feed on your finesse. Here, with a Chinese Chippendale corner cupboard, who is your peer. And a mahogany chair worthy of you. And old-style round playing cards to grace your touch. Here, in beauty—where you are our home.

Woods: mahogany and pine
Date: circa 1820
Place: New Brunswick Museum, Saint John

Marble Mantlepiece

 A way of life is passing in Canada: a way of life that is romantic, graceful, warm and affectionate or sentimental. A way of life that spoke of flowers in a long garden, Wordsworthy poetry, children who could (fortunately) "be seen and not heard"... and a wingchair by the fireplace. Call it the genteel way of life. What used to be thought of as the way of the Christian Gentleman; a way defined by the life of Sir Thomas More, or—closer to Canada—Sir William Osler.

Here this old Romantic way can still be seen, assembled round the marble mantlepiece of Donald and Mrs. MacKay, in Halifax. The mantle itself is a late Georgian piece. Donald says it is pure Adamesque. I think of it as Empire or Regency. What does matter is the fineness of the piece, the crispness of the incised marble carving, the simple (and noble) strength of the pillars—fit centre to a room. Holder of Brother Fire. And upholder of the cut-glass Victorian girandoles, similar in style to some shown at the Great Exhibition of 1851. Holding also the small porcelain figurines, and that full silver bowl of flowers, yes, from the MacKay's garden, which is in itself an essay in Chinese sentience and meditation (full of saxifrage and succulents, and hens-and-chickens, along with carnations and pinks). Over the mantle is a painting (also in the Canadian Romantic tradition of the Group of Seven) done by Mrs. MacKay. Flanking it are miniatures of eighteenth and nineteenth century personages.

"The mantle came originally from Dr. Almon's home, on the corner of Prince and Argyle," Donald is saying. "It was built around 1790. Here is a sketch I did of it.... Almon was Surgeon General to the British Forces here. I got the mantle from his great-great-grandsons. It was one of the Almons, you know, who was Officer of the Day at the Citadel, when they shot a real load from the Noon Gun. Back in World War I... it was an accident. But it was a twelve-pounder and flattened part of a house, about a mile from the Citadel... they later made him Aide to the Lieutenant Governor. Provided, of course, he never used real shot again...."

"This mantle... it's really a whole style of life, Donald. And in our time, it has not merely been replaced, it has been systemically destroyed... hasn't it?" I ask.

There was a quiet pause. And then Donald turned and looked me direct in the eye, as though I had (at last) asked the forbidden question, and as though he wanted for ever to pass some information through me. And in the gentlest and firmest way possible, he said, "Yes Scott... we have been systematically destroyed."

Almost certainly this mantle was made in England, and like hundreds of others, shipped throughout the world of "the Christian Gentleman," not as a mark of "status," but as an affirmation of taste.

Material: white marble
Date: about 1810
Place: home of Dr. Donald and Mrs. MacKay, Halifax

Carved Indian Hunter

Log cabin, snake-rail fence, stumping and barn raising bee; wood-runners (coureurs de bois), fur-traders, Indian-hunters: the wild frontier—all a part of the early Canadian fact: but never the dominant fact as in the early Thirteen Colonies or in the Manifest Destiny of the United States. In French Canada, Church and Court were potent and left their mark of magnificences and political corruption. In English Canada, the British Raj imposted a certified constraint that effectually prevented or at least delayed the mere material rape of the Dominion. Meditation and manners—Church and Crown—modern Canada wants to overlook the truth, that it is these which gave us a very different birth and culture from that of the United States!

But if very secondary, sheer Americanism was still important in early Canada: Sam Slickery, the American squatters agitating in early Ontario, New England settlers opening up the Eastern Townships of Québec as part of a greater New England.

Here is a fine example of the American Dream within Canadian culture, complete with buckskin coat, powder horn, moccasins, Kentucky rifle, feather headdress. This Indian Hunter is at once a valid echo of Cooper's Leatherstocking and of Davy Crockett, King of the Wild Frontier. He is possessed both of the feline grace of the Redskin and the paleface grace of the American concept of Nature's Nobleman. And he has something of the limpidity of a fine English Wedgwood plaque or a marble statue by Canova, which dates and places him. Almost life size, he was housebroken and originally stood in a parlour in Victorian Saint John. I wanted to set him free, so we took him outside in the sun and snow and sky and photographed him —as a latter day Statue of Liberty.

John Graham, who worked in Crouchville, New Brunswick, in the second quarter of the nineteenth century, carved this statue. He and his son Robert and a grandson, also Robert, created ships' figure-heads, statues, tobacconists' signs, and a variety of other carved works. They formed a dynasty of craftsmen, rather like the Levasseurs or the Baillargés of French Canada. But while most of the French Canadian carving was for the Church, most of the best Maritime carving must have been for ships, especially figure-heads.

Very little survives. A pair of simplified Corinthian capitals here, a bird or a wild animal there (with all the precision of a Colville painting), a statue of Gladstone or a rampant Scot in full regalia or a big-busted Queen Victoria nursing an entire Empire. . . . We can only surmise its beauty and quality from a statue such as this; most Maritime carving has now gone the way of the wooden ships.

Wood: pine
Date: about 1830
Place: New Brunswick Museum, Saint John.

Pictou Portal

The overt form of this substantial pine doorway is late eighteenth century English Adamesque. The fanlight, the urns atop the side columns, the bevelled panels, the reeding, and the "sun's rays" over the fanlight: all of these are in the neo-classic tradition which was essentially (in England at least) an intellectual and cultural achievement of the aristocracy.

Yet we recognize that this vigorous doorway, so ostensibly neo-classic Enlightenment in form, is in fact something quite other. It is the very ebullience of this door which leaves us anything but "detached." We can try to flatten it out, tie it down, with our appreciative eye . . . but it keeps bouncing back— and aristos just *don't* bounce! There is definitely some kind of flow and spring and . . . and flesh to this door. Maybe it's those large suns, maybe it's those forms above the urns, suspiciously like fish! Maybe it's the distending deep-carved angel-wings over the fan. . . . The late Georgian form—the High Style Aristocrat—and the bounce and bustle of the piece, these come together and fuse. And it is this which is definitive to the door, making it unique, making it someone particular.

Who? Just Who is this "person" combining with such warm precision, such reasonable embodiment, both the bouncing bod of folk and the detached mind-full eye of the eighteenth century aristocrat?

It can't be European: there the folk did not ape their betters with such nonchalance; nor did the European bourgeois retain such pith. It isn't New England: not enough asperity and too much flesh (damnable!). Though it might be early Connecticut there is yet something too militantly massive about it, something too British. Nor is it French Canadian: it is too reasonable, too balanced—it never takes off! It is neither so garrulously folk nor so gaudily High as the best French Canadiana!

And finally, it is not early Ontario: there is something too imaginative about it, something too gusty and gutsy.

No. This doorway comes from the famous Twelve Mile House of West River—in its day the greatest hostelry east of Halifax—near Pictou, Nova Scotia.

This harmonious fusion of firm yet frolicking folk and dignified responsible squire—the blending at once of the common people and the man of quality: what Thomas Haliburton did with Sam Slick and Squire Poker; and what the Nova Scotians did as a people. Even today the Maritimers have it—a sense of sentient presence, in the flesh and mind and eye....

Wood: pine
Date: about 1830
Place: Nova Scotia Museum, Citadel Hill, Halifax.

Victorian Rococo Chair

 Those Victorian ladies, going to church! In high bonnets and bustles. Their heads round with curls of coils, their shoulders sloped demurely (a shawl!), their busts bulging and tapering almost abruptly: Wasp Waist (how *did* the race survive?).

Almost gala, with ribbons for the young. And fans for the elegant.

And almost merely stern... like the churches themselves, with their sharp-pinnacled asperity and stolid bodies clomping the ground.

Louella Creighton tells of these ladies and their times in her book, *The Elegant Canadians*... a title whose very choice tells us that we must have forgotten or misplaced or displaced that "elegance."

And, lest we should think that such stern curvaceous Victorian elegance is a myth or a lie or a faint-hearted nostalgia, here is this chair—which is replica, in the flesh, of such ladies (and their gents). Here is the swelling bosom, and the tapered waist, clenched in its gut, taut. Here is the full thigh. We have forgotten women of fertile thighs as we watch of streets populous of females who walk brittle like mannekins; and men who talk like women! We have forgotten Reubens' flanks and Diana of Ephesus.

Lest we forget that some other vision of life and fecundity is or ever was possible, here is this Victorian chair, combining deep-earth fertility and some kind of chastity (hard to put your finger on). A carnal Madonna....

Here is this rococo side chair—at once young and buxom... and also old, in her seat of satin—your grandmother or mine, or great-great-grandmother. Sitting planted forever behind her potted ferns. Is she in her golden oaken parlour, complete with needlework (working a portrait of the Queen—Victoria—enwreathed with maple leaves)? Or is she in some endless hotel lobby, one of the great trans-Canadian châteaux, built especially to cater to her strong romantic dream: Château Frontenac, or Banff Springs, or Château Lake Louise, or the Empress in Victoria—is she lobby-sitting, watching her world stroll by... commenting with sweet malicious glee on every buck and lass (and some sadness of her own, remembered)? Or is she at church—Methodist, I believe—the potted ferns still there—watching Uncle Charlie pump the organ and playing Rock of Ages just off key?

Here she is, gussied up—born in Prince Edward's Island well before Confederation... she rightly wears the Prince's plumes at her waist and has some touch of spud-rife earth.

Wood: tiger maple
Date: about 1850
Place: Nova Scotia Museum, Citadel Hill, Halifax

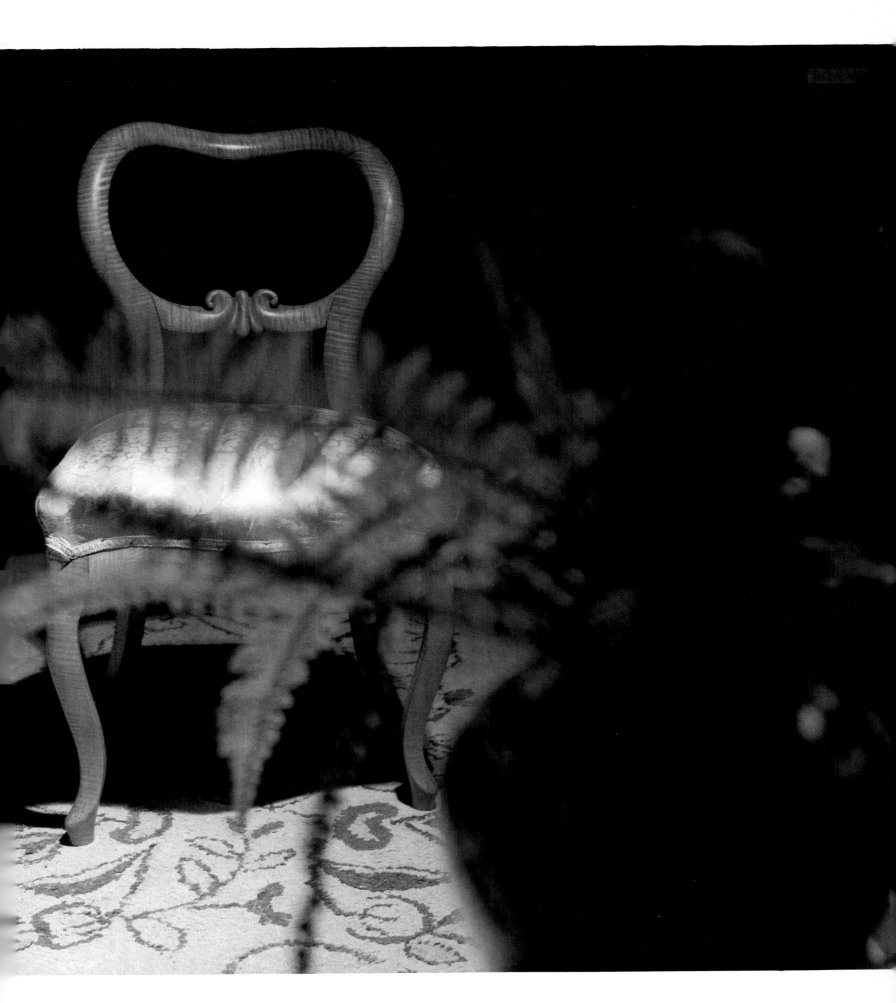

High Victorian Piano

Somewhere in our common folk-memory, a picture of Prince Albert standing slightly off to the right side, and looking ineffably svelte (and wasp-waisted, as well). A bevy of officials, protocollared and clean shaven (even if wearing beards, they feel so hairless!). Palm trees and giant ferns and a great oak rising from the plush-carpeted floor to a sky of glass—ensheathing the group of officials. And in the centre, looking like a lily, a lady's slipper, and her own Annunciation, Girl-Queen, at once virgin to the eye and yet Mother of nine children, and Mother of the Mother of Parliaments and of The Greatest Empire The World Has Yet Seen—QUEEN . . . Victoria. Opening officially the Great Exhibition of 1851, in her people's Palace of Crystal.

It was the golden age of such sumptuous exhibitions, and craftsmen and companies from all over the world sent their lush wares to display virtuoso capabilities.

In Canada, one William Fraser won first prize at the Nova Scotian Exhibition of 1854 for his fine furniture. By 1862, his sons received good mention at the London International Exhibition . . . for their pianos. And in 1867 they could send a masterpiece such as this carved piano to the Paris International Exhibition, where it received a special prize.

It must have made a magnificent sight—with its cascade of tightly carved bird's-eye maple, and its purple velvet backing behind the rococo foliation.

Even today, with its velvet largely gone and the cover to the keyboard lost, it stands like some High Altar; complete with reredos and stuffed relics—in this case a companion survival piece, of Victorian birds.

Yes, High Altar it is . . . virtuoso visual fugue—palpable presence from an Empire. Compare it with that other Canadian High Altar, carved a century earlier, for Notre Dame Church, in Place d'Armes. Both pieces are essentially the same form—baroque bodies . . . full foliate rococo carving.

But the Notre Dame Altar is something which grows from within itself; its body swelling with natural pride of majesty. And its carving is the flower of this exuberance. Whereas this piano is (finally) something mightily concerted. It is an act of will-power . . . something "built"—like a fort. It does not really undulate or curve. And its rococo carving is squared right into the body, at once contained, and at the same time constraining, like cast iron.

It *commandeers* my admiration!

Wood: bird's-eye maple
Date: 1867
Mark: William Fraser and Sons, Halifax
Place: Nova Scotia Museum, Citadel Hill, Halifax.

New Brunswick Indian Quillwork

 The Indians metaphored the land!

In the far west, on the lush, fern-deep, rain-rich coast, the Haida Indians created villages whose very homes embraced tree-trunks 50, 100, 150 feet high...totems—they were a kaleidoscope of surrounding nature. Like their carved soft-stone plates, boxes, pipes...so that the eye leaps and swoops and laughs, with frog, eagle, and raven.

Or on the prairies, men walked whose clothes were the skin of Brother Bear, or Sister Deer—paid for, not at Holt Renfrew's, but by ritual dance, acknowledgement in the blood and body. While men chanted with guttural throats like early morning marsh—bittern, rail, geese.

And the prairie needlework, quillwork, beadwork, has a starkness of bright greens, blues, reds, that are a prairie sunrise and the song of Western Meadowlark—quite unlike either colour or sound further east.

And in each of Ontario and Québec there is the influence of the land...and of English and French cultures, respectively. So that you find Indian Chiefs dressed up marvellously, looking like some combination of Red Tailed Hawk, Aztec Priest, Natty Bumppo, and the Prince Regent. For example, the self-portrait of Theolariolin, known also as Zacharie Vincent, in Québec. Or the Romney portrait of Thayendenaga. Chief Brant—complete with Tomahawk, and ceinture flêchée!

And here, this rich quill mat by nineteenth century New Brunswick Indians...is New Brunswick. The high hills and sloping Green Mountains. The float of gull, the bleak of crow against the snow, the woodland flowers (dog-tooth violets). Such Maritime quillwork mats and boxes and baskets just are *not* prairie eyes, nor do they have the natural rococo, "chinoiserie," of the "oriental" Haida work.

Somehow the Indians embodied the land...in their person, their few material possessions, and in their walk. In contrast Ontario houses (and people) walk *on* the land, immobile even as they move. And Ontario furniture is without colour (it has a glow, a sheen, a tone...but not colours!). Québec decor has some of the colours the Indians saw and transferred to their own persons. And Québec furniture has the rare salmon or rooster or pine tree...rampant. And the Maritime furniture has the roll of the sea, and the seat of the Yankee saddle....

But no mere white man has sung the song of the land as well as these simple quillworked Indian objects do! And until we do...we'll strangle in our own identity!

Date: late 19th century
Place: New Brunswick Museum, Saint John

Gateleg Dining Table

 Wait a minute! What are you doing?

During the very time you've been writing this table off, as immobile, thickset, ponderous and tombstone-ish, you've moved up to it—your hands are on top! Not just fingertips, as with Ontario maple-tables, but your whole hand, palms cupped full down—grateful.

And your whole body yearns for a chair, short, to mate the shorty height of the table. Almost a nursing chair height. So that as you sit, you are rolled over intimate with yourself, huddling and

"Who's that feeling my leg? Under the table!"

And you reach down, careful not to look, and grasp the round bulbous thick yet moving...hand moving down...the table's leg itself, against yours. That leg you thought was so steadfastened, so merely stolid, it ripples full to the hand. You look down, to make sure—and yes the whole underthigh of the table *is* in motion. All those thickset muscles flowing. You put your hand back on top, to stabilize and note that the top, too, flows with rounded corners.

Too late you want to jump back, out, and away. But now you are part of the table. You note that your ears are humming...strumm-sound...bass-viol, violin with a throat to it, violin with virility.

While your host serves you cretons and an earth-

crock of vin du pay...is it grape? And the memory lurches back of a small parish church, upslung from the hugging ground, tangled with vines, in the Basque country where the French taureaux fight. And you know, oh you know, that Kriegoff told his truth. Because you are Jolifou, you too are jocund with that touch of flesh that goes beyond English merriment to the Mass!

This French Canadian's table, with its Henri Quatre (Paris *was* worth a Mass!) heft in the turned legs, though the turnings are closer to Louis XIII, while the "trumpet form" of the middle segment of these leg is Louis XIV (remember? that portrait by Rigaud?). The curved top is probably mid eighteenth century, and the whole piece could have been made as late as 1830. But in fact is probably early eighteenth century. A country carry-over.

This box-that-moved...you. Something like Chinese script, the earth-and-rock-and-pine landscape in flight, with warblers—and the memory of winter past (thank God....

Wood: pine
Date: early 18th century
Place: Montréal Museum of Fine Art

Flame Finial Table

 If the preceding table is vin du pays and cretons (pig's-trimmings in their own fat! try them!—at Les Trois Guinguettes, in le Vieux Quartier, Montréal), this one is a mature Burgundy, rich full red-bodied, drunk from a blown and stem-knopped glass.

If the preceding table is a bass-viol, this is a French horn, *plus* violin and cello.

If that last table is Krieghoff's Jolifou Inn, this is a Court case. Take off your Phrygian toque…look for the Cardinal's hat. Because here is no country Church upheld by visions of the Virgin in the eyes of some rustic maid amilking: here is a Cathedral!

If the Habitant table had trumpet-turned legs with Henri Quatre mass, this one has full, deeply turned and deeply turning legs, whose very spiral cannot be contained within the sheer legs themselves but overflows (joyous occasion!) into those coiled flames at each end, and on into that utterly gratuitous central tochère … an uprising in its own right!

If the folk table had curved corners, rounding off some kind of box-that-moves, this one has full-bodied ballet. You cannot keep it down.

And if the other was firm earth-brown, this has that full oxblood-and-aged red:

Oh yes—with its generous spirallings and its richness of colour, its mass and its strength, combined so fluently in powerful baroque dance, this table is typical of furnishings created at Bishop Laval's Ecole des Arts décoratifs, founded at Cap Tourment, near Québec City, about three full centuries ago, when the Stuarts were still England's Kings—and Faith was Imagination still True—the "long Newtonian sleep" had not yet begun.

Such pieces were for a Church and Court, finer, fuller and gaudier (despite Laval's Jansenism) than any living art north of an equally-Catholic Mexico.

Probably for a Monastery or Nunnery, this table resembles those saved from the fire in the Hôtel-Dieu of Montréal in 1695.

Wood: birch and pine (top replaced)
Date: about 1690
Place: Canadiana Gallery, Royal Ontario Museum

Diamond-Point Buffet

I go into the Montréal Museum seeking some overall insight in-to French Canadians —are they mitigated French? Improved French? Or British North American French? Trudeau often looks, acts, like the last Battle of Britain pilot. . . .

. . . not going bluntly into the Québec gallery, but turning away, circling warily—past early Greek vases with forever atheletes and modest maidens . . . simply nude . . . prancing like pure Pans: Eros was not denied.

And the Medieval Illuminations: pages shimmer like stained-glass windows, illuminating me.

And richly inquisitorial fifteenth century doors and Spanish coffers, eternal tumescence, kinder in their beauteous and blatant tyranny than the puritan plush that is mod architecting.

And heaven-sized triptychs of Virgin, Holichild, and Spirit—three-in-one, inseparable to my eye they create: humane triangle, Trinity, engulfed in blood and gold, silent and still. The passers-by are shadows.

And just beyond, loud horn and horseman questing wildebeaste within the very eye of God, are tapestries, I see.

Beside these, eighteenth century English porcelain, rows of it, is wan, bled white . . . the Reign of Reason was a leech. And Matthew Arnold wept dry tears on Dover Beach.

And I swing round now, past ferocious cthonic statuary from Mitla's Mexico and (cousins, these) serpentine sculpting that is tundra and whale-teeth, Eskimo.

And, feral, penetrate the French Canadian gallery, on the eyeballs of my rising hope and, ahhh, feel it in one fell swoop. . . .

Implanting myself in front of the first piece I can . . . Blue Buffet . . . I almost stare at this cupboard as at some detached, isolated piece. But at the very moment my mere-mind might try to "detach, label, and file," the cupboard grapples me into touch. Approaching my eye with what *may* seem only three-dimensional perspective, this object in fact leaps out at me, does not simply recede . . . it circles and flows like the curved bevelling around the diamond-doors and the deep curve in the crowning pediment and the encircled handles with open hearts . . . even the keyhole escutcheons are arabesqued gothic, halberds.

And these escutcheons are microcosms of the entire piece: which catches the eye as square and Renaissance, but *does* to me what medieval illuminations do, rising and swarming all over, imbedding me warm and whole as in a Cathedral. This is a metaphor from the great Cathedrals of the Middle Ages, and *they* were microcosms of the entire world, embracing man as he devoured God in the chalice.

Wood: pine
Date: about 1725
Place: Montréal Museum of Fine Arts

Baroque Bed

Along the Grande Allée, past the small home Krieghoff lived in, through the fields of the Battle of Abraham, past the busbied Citadel, through the great stone gates of Québec City—Canadian Carcasonne, and along past Kent House, and into Québec's Place d'Armes...with the Château Frontenac rising in superb visual culmination of the Cape. And to my left the Anglican Cathedral of the Holy Trinity, still celebrating its serene Palladian God. And on, down past Claude Baillif's seventeenth century tower—checking to make sure the Rooster is still atop (yes . . . chanticleer . . . clear-song). And duck in-to Laval's great courtyard; the taut, stern, ordered face of Canadian Jansenism—intact.

Thence down the ramparts overlooking the Ile d'Orleans and along to the Hôtel-Dieu, still carrying on its work of God three centuries on, knock at the door, admitted by a Sister in habit. "I came to see. . . ."

There, rising to my cornered eye, the spirals, the great flesh—clotted rising spirals, that are the baldaquin by Bolvin in the Church at Neuville; and, in Bishop Bourget's Cathedral in Montréal, the baldaquin which is a half-size replica of the one in St. Peter's in Rome—and in St. Peter's itself, Bernini's great Baldaquin that is the Glories of Greece and Rome, visual Aquinian reality . . . a world in résumé, with Michelangelo's terribilata of soul sown in the monumental marble and the Mass.

And the Sister is all smiles, saying, "That is a guest bed. They say that the Marquis de Frontenac slept in it. . . ."

But I am gone on beyond . . . beyond the blue curtains which Peter Kalm noted two centuries ago —like Faience ware with the birch of the bed . . . beyond this museum, beyond the matters of the mere-mind, beyond academic fiction or romantic fact. These centripetal pillars have wound me up and up, have caught me up in some kinetic creation of energies, which has penetrated the still core of me and torn my brain loose from its concrete foundation and whorled me till the Sister spins in front of me, her words like butterflies, bright amidst the Chicory and I want to laugh in such delight. And suddenly it is all still and I hear the Sister again—her face is very beautiful, like Plamondon's Mère Sainte-Anne. And I realize that this bed is an unstated concept of Incarnation— defining me across mere centuries. That it sweeps everything up, the flesh rising — everything in touch, everything so compenetrant, nothing isolated—no severances. I understand the phrase, that "all flesh shall see it together." And I know that the bed has taken me through some orgy of the eye and released me into a new, this "other," world . . . wedding me unto a new reality: Magnified.

Wood: birch
Date: late 17th century
Place: Collection de la Musée de l'Hôtel-Dieu, Québec

Church Carving

(Saint Michael and the Dragon)

Each one amuttering, and then, as you kneel, become a rroar, silent surf from behind the inner ear. And this rroar bows your head but opens your inner eye, so that every word said is as limpid as sparkle by diamond light. A New World, a New Dimension of being. Open, wide opened . . . the opposite of all that is taut tight, the opposite of all that is purse-lipped and merely precise. A completely renewed World, so different from wasp-waist or any mode of coitus interruptus. A world full of grace and gentle-ness. A world whose mere secular counter-part is gentility.

AVE . . . .

Just so, like candles in a church, these roses round the columns carved around the flaming dragon worthy of death at the hands of Michael, Archangel and Saint.

Just so, like roses bound around a rising column the soft seraphim of Michael's face, the luscious turn of his embodied torso, around a force of steel. (Evil can never succeed, because if it did it would be Good, against itself.)

Just so, like sweet seraphim of Saint Michael's face,

this Dragon-of-All-Evils (Satan incarnate) . . . this very Dragon-of-Evil has a mild ferocity as if the hand who carved this piece could not entirely grasp Evil—but simply symbolize it.

Just so, like some sweet and Heaven-sent Dragon, this group of carvings for l'Eglise de l'Ange Gardien, this Saint Joachim school of craftsmen—this rétable which presents the entire world of Louis XIV (his portrait by Rigaud is simply this Michael in worldly drag).

Just so, this Altar-group, who, in worldly terms is provincial baroque, French, sugar-dipped in Regency, with its Marco Polo dragon like some fat Buddha poodle proving only that at two removes Chinoiserie touched eighteenth century Canada.

Just so, this Ange-Gardien, an academic curio—easy to label it, yet if you kneel, the roses rroar, the Dragon flames, and Michael is a Saint with wings . . . .

Wood: pine
Date: about 1700
Place: Musée provinciale du Québec

Os du Mouton Armchair

1776. The American Revolutionaries have captured Montréal and all but captured Québec. The Manifest Destiny of these New Romans to rule (if not the world) America at least seems clear. Benjamin Franklin sits in state on a dais in the Château de Ramezay, home of the governors, French and then English, of Montréal and of Canada. And he exhorts the French Canadians to fight for their liberty, alongside the Americans.

Good old Ben! Did he wear his coonskin cap, as he did at Versailles?—he's Nature's portly nobleman, crackerbarrel Voltaire. Except that he was probably spouting quasi-Christian platitudes à la *Poor Richard's Almanac* — and these to the Canada born of Jeanne le Ber and Mère Marie de l'Incarnation and Brébeuf and Laval!

Well, Brother Benjamin could not convince the French Canadians of the purity of Greater New England, of its Myth and the Second Adam. A sentient observer might easily have predicted he could not. Because Ben probably sat in a chair like this one!—not in an American Windsor chair as all those Signers of Independence did, as Ben himself did in Pine's famous painting, not in an American whorlwind Windsor at all, but an Os du Mouton chair similar to this: with its warm swoop of wood, flowing, arching birchwood curving and cusping, its nobility of back, tall and broad, its velvet or Turkey point or crewel-worked seat. . . .

See Ben sitting in a chair like this, fidgeting uneasily in all its pride, flare, and prance, high hip and Cavalier. Chair like those men Van Dyke painted— since classic Greece have men ever been so beautiful and at the same time so sensitive? Well, here is good old Ben sitting edgily in one of their chairs. Was he remembering that the Roundheads cut off King Charles' head for being so fine? And did the French Canadians recognize him as a latter-day Roundhead?

The French Canadians watching this conflict between sapient Ben and their Chair of All Majesty, the real representative plenipotentiary of their culture, the King being absent, these men must have sensed some unbending asperity, some hidden barbed-wire brittleness, beneath the bright American banalities, some rumour of totalitarian rule by moral recipe, by reproval and by rebuke: Holy Protestant Democracy. Yes. They sense, at the ends of their fingertips, some shrivel-minded utilitarianism, some tight-eyed wit of conceit, which they cannot put into a phrase. They watch Benjamin sit in their chair.

And the chair phrases all their feelings for them. This chair with its French royal bleu ciel, its glister of studs, this chair at once courtier and martyr and saint—with its Crown of Thorns, this regal Canadian chair in native birch says precisely how and why Benj. Franklin and the American Dream were ejected by the French Canadians.

Wood: birch
Date: 1700-1760
Place: Château de Ramezay, Montréal

Japanned Buffet

Coldwind searing le Vieux Quartier. Ice stabbing down from the high eaves of the Ville Marie (the memory fresh, of de Gaulle in majesty, proclaiming Québec libre!) Behind me the old Monument to Nelson—the first in the world.

Duck into the Château de Ramezay, residence of Governors . . . duck in, and going I know where. To the room at the far end. To feast my eyes and warm my winter-heart in that Buffet. All those flames and floral outbursts. Cornucopia of black and gold—Oriole . . . "the gold one." Some kind of controlled holocaust you are. Kindling me; my eyes caught in the grape clusters of your panels that are flowers. Caught and revolving and—P H O O O S H—I'm shot clean to your topknot . . . up your central gold trunk, in blossom, riding in blossom across your top, some foliate vine.

Oh yes! You ARE the Sun King. I stand before you. No thought of seeking a seat. No thought of talk. High silence—that is what you wanted, isn't it, Roi Soleil—You wanted us to be dazzled, stunned into our open-eyed silence? Like Louisbourg—some palace rising from the rocks, to stun the enemy into acquiescence!

And as I stand I note my ears ahumming. That hum which comes when you are listening to the song of first Spring Robin, as unexpected, he pierces your Winter-sealed ears and caverns open . . . like side chapels in a closed Cathedral. Reverberations. A new dimension. So, now, I know I expect more . . . some door to open (Sesame you are . . . and I truant thief of your French gold). Yes—more to come—and I enabled, by you, if it does

Strange. You are like that double-cupboard in blue—you both focus my mind and soar it. But you grapple me a step further. You . . . ahh!—I have you . . . YOU ARE THE ALLELUIA CHORUS. You create my faith as you demand it. All I have to do is submit to your beauty, your munificence. "Submit!"—the hardest thing for Western Man, Western Protestant Man, to do. Submit, I must . . . to beauty.

Oh—I know—an academic text would say that you are merely a seventeenth century Baroque Cupboard, a provincial piece, a take-off of the Court Style, your black-and-gold but poor-man's japanning. You—a mere vestment cupboard from the sacristy of the old Church in Trois Rivières. Circa 1775. Probably made by those Flemish craftsmen the Bishop imported . . . An "anthropological curiosity" as one distinguished professor said (he's dead now, cancer of the brain).

But to me, you are grounds for Celebration . . . your rich rococo floral elegances, your Baroque bust, your voluted legs each an altar in themselves. Your flowers that *do* flower (flowering me . . .).

Your final levitation of mass. Oh yes, you are elegance and panache, implanted here, on the banks of the Sainted Lawrence two centuries back.

You are a promise . . . which I must keep. Ahh—I see I give myself away. Why not?—to thee. I am a Romantic—a Romantic who has paid his dues. Therefore I rejoice . . . .

Wood: butternut
Date: about 1775
Place: Château de Ramezay, Montréal

Habitant Armoire

the fish, the prancing deer, the sun-circled pine, cock atop, the rising vine, the chalice feeding all

seeing this deep-carved habitant armoire, like some Indian totem come live, stirs a memory:—

it was at Lac Trois Saumons. The glint of bright on my face, as I wake and topple out to the edge of the lake. Tripping over vines and my own stubbed bare feet. Just in time to surprise the sun rising over the mountain thigh, and the splatter of fish jumping clear of the mirrored sun and—tumbling back—scattering the sun in a thousand rings that tickle my toes. Ahh—it needs only a rooster to crow, and I wait—but none (terribly tempted to fill its place).

And we are up, and once again en route—pursuing early furniture clean across Eastern Canada.

Saint-Aubert…fine nineteenth century Church, making hewn stone sing.

Sainte-Louise…along the backroads above the Big River we can feel, but only rarely see between the marble hills, a string of farm homes revealing exactly their date and culture of birth

—a flared eave and Norman stance
—a flurry of English Adamesque fan-work over front door
—a turgidity of verandah verging and posts (Scottish Victorian Byzantine—to be precise!)
—a carved neo-classic pediment that belies the mere-mind who

BRAKES…ply the brakes: across the front of our truck, prancing high, ears cocked and antlers carrying the land, pine trees and sun. The large buck

pauses briefly to gaze at us gaping at him…and wanders off

Saint-Gabriel,

Saint-Pacôme

and crossing criss-crossing under us, the frothing turbulence of la Rivière Ouelle

one small town celebrating its own centennial with home-carved statues of Christ and Moose and Maple Leaves and Christmas lights for ever

A Church looming to our right, massive, twin towers added or aggrandized (that spiritual trade-mark of Québec)—and a cock *does* crow and we start to laugh, gleeing laughter. And pull up—is it because of cockcrow or the church? or both? And cross the paved square to the frontal high-arching over us and the white wooden urns atop—and breach this stone entry and…ohhh—suddenly in some celestial city of silences—gold and white, vines and palm leaves and angels' wings suspending us with them inside this barrelled vault, this pocket basilica proclaiming communion and celebration.

the fish, the prancing deer, the cock acrow, the chalice and the vine of life.

This armoire and that day of joy, one and the same. I turn to our host. "Where did that Armoire come from?"

"The Gaspé…Rivière Ouelle"

Wood: pine
Date: late 18th century
Place: home of Mr. Edgar Davidson, Cushing, Québec

Armchair à la Canadienne

 . . . remember when you first put your arms around me. In the Ile d'Orleans home of artist energumen, Claude Picher. We were in full agape, eating perdrix au chou and wild rice, with a 1951 Château Ausone. When Claude shot bolt upright and called for a "trou normand"—that intermission in a meal which is a shot-glass of Calvados drunk neat, so that the throat roasts and a hole is drilled through your stomach to accommodate more food.

I lurched happily up from the table and toppled into your undulant arms. And found my fingers wandering your rolling, turning, roiling arms, legs, seat. Fingers turning with your expanding walnut flesh, caught at the rim of yet another tip, top, knop—and a ludicrous smile of ecstasy that. . . .

"MAUDITS ANGLUCHES, VOUS ETES CONSTIPES. . ."
—Claude roaring benignantly at me.

I felt some anger, consternation, at Claude's taunts, and also at this way I was lolling in your arms, undignified, finger-tippling. And I extricated myself from your arms, as though somehow I had been *had*—some part of me touched that must absolutely not. . . .

"THAT CHAIR, HE LIKES YOU, 'TI ANGLUCHE, 'TI CUL CARRE"—Claude leering like some heavenly Mephistopheles through the added perspective of the Calvados. My wife managing a wan smile, while eyeing you as possible encroachment on our marriage I could not understand but knew.

That was in 1959—my core attained. My smug opacity ended.

I learned later that you are called a "Salamander Chair" for unknown reasons; in French "une chaise à la capucine," after your cowled back-rails, like a Capuchin monk's hood.

I learnt, too, that there is no chair style precisely like you in France—or anywhere else. And I began to recognize you as definitive, with your Louis Treize turning legs, and your full-embodied form virtually Louis Quatorze, and all your gaiety and elegances recalling the Régence and Watteau's Voyage to Cythera; and your arms, Louis Quinze rocaille. I realize that you were somebody unique.

I started my quest for you. And each time I found you, I knew again you were some-body—with your folk Catholic forms. And your peasant ebullience, yet your high courtliness . . . till one day I accepted you as the French Canadian par excellence—you, the habitant made good! With your Medieval roots, your Renaissance and Baroque faith, and your French rococo manners—plus post-Conquest affluence. You kept everything together. Perfect case of cottage-King. I rejoiced with you.

And then, in 1964, we heard that there were a dozen of you in Montreal, available. You came dear—at a thousand dollars a head. But your vitality was necessary (my wife's dead grandfather paid). And we set you around our twelve-foot Refectory dining table, also from Québec. And watched you always alive, moving, conversing, laughing—yet serene. Quick, and not born into some still-life. We called you (in private) the Twelve Apostles.

I bought a large Crucifix, from the Gaspé, to complete you. Already you were "inadmissible evidence"—some kind of carnal rosary, confuting the Ontario Matriarch in the Mink Coat and high (sharp) heels, and Birks Blue Box.

You see, in the end, you won in me. Or, as Jacques Godbout warned me long ago—"you'll have to become a French Canadian to survive!" And I did.

Woods: walnut and maple
Date: end of the 18th century
Place: Canadiana Gallery, Royal Ontario Museum

Bow-Front Commode

Ontario furniture never moves—except en bloc, all its energies pent in the wood. The flaming maple locked in.

Contrast this slowly firmly seething flank of flesh—warm, at once robust and pullulant. The tiger stripe of inner maplewood caught and carried in some potent life-ballet, celebrant. . . .

This chest-of-drawers is no block-house (and no blocked life) but presents at once the cudding comfort of brown cow, grazing udder-deep in meadow grasses sown with shining marigolds and all the barrel-chested pride of stag with full antlers—only this is more robust—Moose, with pendulous dew-lap (Canadensis)

and all the rock-bound stolidity of a Norman farmhouse, yes, but with that intrinsic flowing grace like curving eave (even the outdoor bakehouses in Québec boast this

all the simplicity of earthenware folk—the rich earth-russet of this maple—but with an artisto grown in besides. Potent wedding of land and landlord—consummated (no stalemate here!). Neither a false and forced democracy nor a decadent aristocracy—but the firm embodiment of the people, and the finesse of the marquis.

This piece that is some candid combination, as with so much French Canadiana, of Louis XIV and XV—Sun King, plus flirt (suivez-moi, Monsieur . . . that fillip in the tail!). The cloven hooves, along with the feeling of mass-in-motion, these are Louis XIV. But the particular serpentine front—in French, "arbalète"—literally "cross-bow"—along with the curving skirt, are Régence. While the rear legs are pure Louis Quinze rococo (along with the flashy handles which I presume are mod repro). This run-on of styles is enough to suggest French Provincial. Add the fact that this chest-of-drawers is in full-striped tiger maple, with pine as secondary wood, and you know it could have been created in only one place in the world: French Canada. And in only one period: the second half of the eighteenth century.

Oh—this breast-of-drawers, fusing the figured maple and the flesh of the wood in one flow, is all Québec, and never (no *never*) Ontario.

Woods: curly maple and pine
Date: second half of the 18th century
Place: Montréal Museum of Fine Arts

Original High Altar, Notre Dame de Montréal

I remember when I first came to you, in Place D'Armes. I was writing my first novel (it was writing me—and changing my entire life!). I entered Notre Dame, your church—and was taken aback, by the opulence, the sheer gaudiness. It seemed, to my still astringent eye, "too much"—too ornate. All the carving, the plush of gilt. Without mentioning the chain of Masses hauling God back and forth from the Altar half-a-dozen times a day. No—I could not stomach all that.

But I came back . . . and back. Seeking rest from a stone-grey world. A world of memos (and no real memories). A world of rising competence, and declining celebration. I came back to your church, to rest, just to sit . . . and slowly s l o w l y I allowed my glimpsing eye to wonder about; hooking on the multitude of knops and flying finials, my tired eye clambering, groping a way (amidst the fool's gold, it seemed). While again the Masses played—some ancient Morality Drama, I half-said; and took the guided tour instead.

Till one day I came upon you, in Side Chapel (#3 I think—midway down the Right Ambulatory). And immediately knew you were different from the rest. I suppose you seemed less gaudy. And your flow was from with-in your body—not appliqué. Yes, you were a full-bodied Minuet . . . with your controlled coruscation of carvings. You were serene, yet ebullient. Stable, yet so fluent. Modest, you did not scream at me, for all your beauty (whereas your Church still seemed to shrill). Modest—yet (in some serious way) flirtatious. Courting the attention you create.

I stopped

admiring your features. The carving of the Pelican eaten by her brood, on the door of the Tabernacle (where they kept the Bread). Living sacrifice, that bird giving her very body to her offspring. So crisp and clear it could be work by some spiritual protegé of Michelangelo. Deep in the wood.

This I admired.

And the force of the swags across your chest, and the massive strength of your claw and ball feet. I admired this sheer craftsmanship in you: the Sun King heft, and rococo delicacy—so very French Canadian (I loved). And I said to myself (with a wistful pride—while they changed the Flag by fiat in Ottawa, and I admired your fecund Fleur de lys)—I said "oh, no carving or furniture work in North America can equal such French Canadian pieces for elegance, finesse, force, or total presence"—Real Presence (I almost said—and began, a bit, to understand). One can only kneel, or run away.

Or, another time, I said "this must be the work of the Ecole de Quevillon, about 1750." And the Priest replied, "it is, done for the original church on this site."

And yet again "This is THE piece of Furniture in French Canada, from which all else spring. This Table at which the Last Supper is served."

Then one day I forgot all this . . . and came back, and knelt, and took the bread.

Wood: pine
Date: about 1750
Place: Church of Notre Dame, Place d'Armes, Montréal

Saint-Geneviève Commode

 Imagine that you know a culture, specific in time and place, whose characteristics you have defined—and found unique. These characteristics are:

—some earthy, folk, often virtually medieval, quality

—a European high Baroque—Catholic in faith, and courtly in culture; but in reduced circumstances

—a Frenchness of elegance, often rococo

—some further clear characteristic that is not at all European; sometimes it is North American Indian, sometimes it is English American, sometimes it seems almost Spanish American (but it is usually lighter, less carnally morbid, than Spanish American).

Call it—in general—a free-flow in form, and an immanence in presence

Suppose you also know that this culture has produced specific forms completely unique to itself. In furniture something like the Armchair à la Canadienne. In architecture, something as distinct as the Conefroy Church style—which combines all the above characteristics in one way or another.

Then you could premise that this culture would produce other unique forms. You could, in your eye's mind, envisage it. On this precise basis, let us create a chest-of-drawers which *is* this culture.

It will be down to earth! Not high and mincing off the ground. Almost a squat, a squatter's, quality.

It will have the massiness of the Baroque. But we know it will be smaller and lighter; to fit smaller homes.

It will be finely and rather heavily carved: Catholic. We know that this carving will not be applied (not an afterthought), but a flowing part of the piece as a whole—and the piece itself will flow from within.

So far so good—our piece takes shape and dimension. Add the fact that this chest-of-drawers will be in a local and not an imported exotic wood (we know this from a thousand other cases!)—maple or walnut, or cherry or butternut. We can suspect it will be butternut, because this is the easiest of the finer woods to carve—with (possibly) some of it pine.

But something specific is missing still—some North American quality—ahhh, that's it: this commode will be bow-fronted—Régence or Louis XV—but the centre of the bow will be assertive, even square, a chest-out quality to it.

In the 1930's early collectors of French Canadiana began to find commodes in the Montreal region, a number of which fitted this description. They were quite unlike any commode in the Western (or Eastern) World. After a few years it became clear that these particular commodes originated in or near a small town named Saint-Geneviève. And they thereupon nicknamed this chest the Saint-Geneviève commode. It's the one we have just created!—sumptuous as Versailles, yet as homespun as the old grey mare!

Wood: butternut and pine
Date: about 1780
Place: home of Mr. and Mrs. Eliot Frosst, Montréal

Wallpanelling of Monsignor Briand's Private Chapel

"Now that daylight fills the sky,
We lift our hearts to God on high...."

Often, in the small hours of the first morning, Olivier Briand was in here, on his knees—praying for mercy, and Grace. And praying for his people, conquered and lost to the British Crown. Monsignor, and pontiff of the French Canadian Church after the Conquest of 1759—Olivier Briand still lives in the prayers of reverent French Canadians—and thoughtful English Canadians.

He had his chapel especially built for him after his retirement as Bishop—and used it for personal meditation. Pierre Emond, the sculptor and Church carver, was commissioned to do it, in 1786. And after the bombardment of Québec and Montréal and the many fires, this private chapel remains perhaps the finest panelled room extant in French Canada today. It gives us some idea of what the rooms in the Château de Vaudreuil or the Château de Ramezay must have been like. As well as the woodwork in the original Jesuit church—and many of the lost parish churches.

But it was not simply the wealthiest homes and buildings which were panelled. The homes which had Salamander Chairs also often had panelling in a central room . . . which, like the chairs, combined princely elegance of style with spontaneous folk forms. Panelling to accompany the carving on armoires and bahuts rampant with salmon, roosters, or the barrel chest of some local Minotaur.

In furnishing Monsignor Briand's Chapel, Pierre Emond had the delicacy to carve a flowing Olive Tree around the altar—in honour of the bishop's name: Olivier. Reminder of a world now lost to us. A world in which men and women of any rank stopped to give thanks, in the fields, in the courts, or travelling. We have pictures of this—oil-paintings such as Millais' Angelus—but both the feeling and the forms are lost to us.

Monsignor Briand's Chapel is (in my eyes) the most exquisite panelled room in North America—only the carved woodwork of Gunston Hall, Virginia, seems to approach it. It is also a firm reminder that neither the fur trade nor farming (much less commerce) were at the core of New France—but meditation and prayer and a Heavenly City which has much less to do with flagellation than with celebration.

Nearly two centuries later—Canada's first French Canadian Governor General, Georges Vanier, had a private chapel installed for himself at Government House. The nation did not really know till he died. And then it found out that it loved him.

"The Lord Almighty grant us a quiet night and a perfect end...."

Wood: butternut
Date: 1786
Place: Laval University, Québec City

Chandelier

Floating you head-turvy, about five feet up—multiple antennae. Rotor. Deep green and gold. U.F.O.

An unidentified Flying Object, this chandelier that is anything but crystal. Because crystal, with its glittering translucency, has some right to float. But this chandelier, with its solid mass of carved wood painted such deep green it feels black—this massive chandelier has no right to float. Yet float it does . . . at once substantial and at the same time lighter than air. Inexplicable.

And once you accept its presence it has become (again inexplicable) the centre of the room, with all other objects suspended from it. As though it were the sun and the other pieces of furniture in full-bodied orbit around it whorling.

You look up at it—convinced that somehow or other it must be out of place, *not* French Canadian: *not* part of that merely ribald folksy culture Krieghoff depicted. But even as you scrutinize it you see what it is—with its whorl of wire arms curving, and recall the Salamander Chair and its Baroque full-body of carving that is the counter-curve of a Saint-Geneviève commode, and the wood-filagree work of Paschal Church candles as carved by the Ecole de Quevillon in Montréal.

Yes—that's what this chandelier is: it's the entire French Canadian courtly culture in centripetal orbit. And if such a furniture form as this chandelier did not exist we would have to create it. Because the entirety of French Canadian civilization, with its organic, its embodied, unity, demands such a piece.

Demands this palpable resonant exemplar of French Canadian high folk Baroque. And this chandelier (once your eye is vaulted to the centre of the vortex), this chandelier *is*, in every sense, 'mass-in-motion.' And, using three-dimensional space, but taking you beyond (your very head spinning contentment), it becomes what all best Baroque must—mass-in-celestial-motion: High Mass . . . "This is my Body and Blood, given for you."

Even at the merely secular level, this chandelier becomes an experience that can only be matched in North America, outside of French Canada, in the restored Governor's Palace at Colonial Williamsburg, where European seventeenth century chandeliers (of crystal) glitter in full illumination, and full Chamber Music still plays in Court Dress on a Sunday Evening.

Yes—this is French Canadian folk Baroque par excellence—full hallucinogen. The sheer body of the Baroque, plus the lithe undulance of Louis XV rocaille, while those carved 'pineapples' are Louis XVI in style—one of the relatively rare Louis XVI forms in French Canadiana. Take all this, and you have, once again, a form unique to French Canada. Further corroboration of the culture of a cottage-king!

This one was made by André Achin for the Church of Longueuil.

Wood: pine
Date: 1826
Place: Château de Ramezay, Montréal

Sewing Table

"Mariam . . . would you make me some curtains, for my camper? Like this table-cloth. Bright. . . ."

"Shure! I can do 'e for ya," as she stirs rabbit-stew on the wood stove and the cat chases the dog under a skein of chairs.

"I'd like them bright sun-orange, with a green border, and that vine you've got here."

And in a week Mariam has cut and sewn and crocheted and painted in greens, blues, reds, golds—a dozen curtains, so that my camper is no longer some plastic paradise, but a romp of lilacs, roses, kittens-in-shoes, hearts (like some joyful variant of Victorian graveyard motifs . . . come live).

The scene is in Trout River, Newfoundland outport. But I suddenly remember the rectilinear coverlets in so many homes around Kitchener-Waterloo in Ontario. Coverlets leaping with controlled energies, rose-baskets large as archetypes, or lions rampant (sometimes an American Eagle). And at Ontario Fall Fairs, still, amidst the Harvest pumpkins and pickles, a gather of quilts and cushions with Maple Leaves, Moose and Mother written all over. Scattered throughout Southern Ontario, like some remnant fringe.

And in Québec, in smaller towns, the ragrugs champing at my feet, and springing like a woodland floor of pine-needles. And as well, the splendiferous Altar frontals, of Mère Jeanne le Ber . . . rioting like the Order of the Golden Fleece, and tragic as the Death of God. Wrought in Canadian winters cold, three centuries ago.

Or today, in La Place des Arts in Montréal, or boutiques, tapestries by Micheline Beauchemin, rich as Aztec filagree.

And throughout the Maritimes . . . tea cosies, doilies, table-covers, pot-holders—all the daily events of life, nimbly enshrined in people's lace. So that to touch is to touch deep, with happy care and delight.

A whole culture at their finger-tips, with needles and thread and wool and cloth. So that when I come upon this Québec City sewing table I know who I see. Not some dumpy Victorian dowager who doesn't know whether she is French or English Canadian (in fact, a bit of both—"Franglais"), but a merciful Madonna, sprouting forth lilac and grace, bonnets and frills and space to rest your heart in thanksgiving. . . .

And a week later, Mariam is back.

"I made yez some pilla-cases, and this scarf"—so I reach for my wallet to pay my gratitude away (stupid Mainlander, me).

"Oh noo—ya can 'ave 'e."

Woods: mahogany, with cherry, maple, and pine
Date: about 1850
Place: Canadiana Gallery, Royal Ontario Museum

Rustic Rocking Chair

 a pair of Whitethroat sparrows counter-pointsinging

flowers that are greensheaves and purple at the root of a Black Birch tree whose roots snake high above the ground like a root fence (intertwined coronet!)

thrush gurgling somewhere just beyond the ferns windfluttering like some ptarmigan wing

July morning—about seven—at

Lac de l'est—high up the Québec Gaspé mountains—near the New England border. The lake itself like some enclaved fiord, a world unto itself—the nearest house some miles back. The nearest town twenty-five miles back. As I walk the morning beside the lake (no outboards have penetrated so far: the lake is unsmashed)

the underbrush falls back and, out of the wilds, cattle grazing! And, to my left, a low-slung cabin with a long verandah. Rivulet cleaving the centre of this lost woodland farm. I walk along the rivulet, past piles of rocks cleared for this sudden meadow—to the house, as in some dream for real

awaiting me, on the verandah, arms spread in welcome, gesture of a king, a prelate, a friend—a rustic rocking chair. The kind I often see in rural Québec as I drive the backroads. Long arms, with full-turned handles (a real hand-full). High back with a heart cut out of the top—in the centre. And the seat thonged—like snowshoes

not a Boston Rocker—no Bostonian arms ever spread like this, in embrace (a Catholic gesture—part of Holiness)

nor was any Boston Rocker ever this sky-eyed blue, with red arms

the windows are boarded up, the grass splits the boards on the verandah floor. Where do the cattle come from?

I don't care . . . accepting the rocker's morning invitation, I set me down, thankfully. Just in time to see, over the lake, the sudden soaring swoop, thrash . . . and rising heavy from the deep splash, fish wriggling, an Osprey preying breakfast.

* * *

I had no camera with me . . . and the rocker was not nearly so elaborate as the French Canadian tour de force in this photograph. But it had the same cockiness, the same ebullience, the same open friendliness, and this same combination of peasant rustic, and lively art.

This one here embodies that icon of French Canadiana—the rooster, the chanticleer atop Church spires and wayside crosses. This one is 'ti-coq'—all wattle and squawk . . . Plus some sheer Stuart regality, perhaps via New England high back chairs of the late seventeenth century.

But so long as I live, rocking chairs will be Morning Song, and a walk along Lac de l'est.

Wood: maple
Date: 19th century
Place: home of Miss Barbara Richardson, Ste-Agathe des Monts, Québec

Rustic Queen Anne Table

When the Loyalists streamed across the border from the lost Thirteen Colonies into Canada, in the 1780's and '90's, they often brought with them clothes, kitchenware, and house furnishings. Turned (and burned) out of house and home for supporting a Crown they felt more important than mere Democracy (rather the way a Christian feels that Christ is more important than a President!)—these DPs also frequently carried with them some chosen heirloom, such as a cherished Grandfather clock, or Granny's sewing table.

Thus when they arrived in Canada, they started afresh, with log cabin or frame house. But they carried intact, in their minds and fingers, a way of life already two centuries old in the new world. They just were not merely noble savages! For this reason a small, even squalid, log house might sport a simple but fine table such as this—with its cherry legs carved out in Queen Anne pad feet and its plain plank top in pine. The table might have been brought with the Loyalist or made soon after arrival. And while the Queen Anne foot ends as a style in England around 1725, and in the Thirteen Colonies by the Revolution —I have seen such a pad foot on an English Canadian Empire bed of the 1830's. The style, like the loyalty, lingered on—attractively.

What happened is that the Loyalist (or the American squatter) would build himself a log cabin, to pass through his first Canadian winter. Then in a year or three or ten, it would become a cowbarn or pigsty, or a hired man's house. And a new home would be built of frame and plank. And this home, after a

generation, would be superseded by a larger home still, in stone or brick. It was an interesting case of real "instant culture," in Ontario and English Canada! Starting right from scratch on the land, these Loyalists were not starting from scratch in themselves—either spiritually, emotionally, or culturally. They retained not only their experience of living in America, but also the fundamental elements of an Anglo-Saxon civilization a thousand years old. That was why they came to Canada in the first place—to retain that cumulative civilization, on their own terms. They were willing to be displaced geographically so as not to be displaced in their spiritual being.

A table such as this one—call it "survival Queen Anne"—sums up this spiritual reality that was Loyalist Upper Canada, from 1780 to 1810 or '20. A people poor but proud. A people living in peasant conditions—yet part of a princely culture. A people who gave their lives to remain part of an international civilization, yet determined to rule themselves. It was a unique combination—and a difficult one . . . and one which was resolved in the following generations by the creation of a political party called both "progressive" and "conservative"—the party which is particular to Ontario yet representative of a continuing culture in Canada.

Wood: cherry and pine
Date: late 18th century
Place: Upper Canada Village

Dropleaf Table

As you enter the room, a glow, an embering warmth, catches your heart as much as your eye. Like entering a room with a smouldering fire on the hearth. Instinctively you enter such warm welcome, without thinking. But you are stopped, your eye abruptly tightened into another focus—sharply: the incisional lines, both within and without—knife-edged like some unexpected wound. Standing you back as though burnt, by dry ice. Your eye is no longer dilated in warmth, but foreclosed, somehow —and sees only in silhouettes! The warm welcome has been superseded by another reality: this table defining itself, at once hot and cold. With a precision that draws your admiration.

Yes—such a fine rapier taper to these legs. And the concise yet also ample drop-leaves (single planks of figured maple). And the overall strictness of line constraining some flame of voluptuousness. Strictness that is in effect some stricture (do *not* smile before you think). And you don't smile.

Thus your affection (and allegiance) seduced—by the warm welcome, and your admiration sharply coerced (and so subtley that you don't have time to be angered, not quite)... you move forward, once again. But now in a tougher-minded scepticism—some disjunction of emotions and mind—which this table has just imposed upon your unsuspecting eye. You move forward warily, and let your fingers touch, just the ends, lest you get stabbed again.

And touching you suddenly see all those sharp-spired churches that stab the Ontario winter sky. Early Presbyterian stone churches, with sharply-squared bodies and little embellishment, save in the choice of stones themselves—and the stricture in the very straightness with which these stones are squared and laid, in contrast with stonework of French Canadian churches, who dance.

Yes—these strong and visually astringent Presbyterian Churches, so different from either Methodist hulk or Anglican elegance.

Like those early Ontario yeoman portraits. Brightly coloured in oils, they nonetheless seem all bleak-and-white—hemlocked with snake rail... visual barbed-wire black against the snow.

Connoisseurs will call this table county Hepplewhite (barnyard Whig!), lingering on in Ontario till 1850. But I call this table "MacCanadian," because it has the lusting asperity that characterizes the Scotch Presbyterian Galbraith describes so well.

Ahhh—that's it: this table characterizes the Scotch Presbyterian of Ontario, our *real* Wasp, Scotchwasp! —at his beautiful-dutiful best. All the flame under the gloss; never gets out. Impasse... of national proportions.

And remembering that very precise dis-junction we have just experienced with this table; the separation of initial emotional warmth and the sharp-eyed mind, at *our* expense... which is how the table achieved its visual autonomy—remembering this, we know something else: these people *did* divide to rule.

Wood: tiger maple
Date: about 1820
Place: Canadiana Gallery, Royal Ontario Museum

County Hepplewhite Sideboard

 that we are all born in log-cabins, a slop-pail away from the chicken-sty

that snake-rail was our Crown of Thorns, opening up a new land; scraping grain from granite under a lowering (Homer Watson) sky

that we were all some kind of high-brow-hayseeds. Hayseeds with some burdensome allegiance to the respectability of Church and Crown (and some hidden deeper allegiance to future affluences!)

that we were all simple sons of the earth, with Mission explicit to build "the True North, strong and free" (McDougal of Alberta, all of us)—an improved Americaland, sans rye.

This is the myth, tacit (and Methodist at that) Canadian myth. Call it the Log-Cabin Myth. Similar in style to the tale that all Australians were progeny of penitentiaries.

But the fact is that there was always another culture in Canada. A culture of sophistications, elegances, poise and literacy. A culture which stretched from Saint John's to Niagara-on-the-Ontario-Lake, and West. Just as it stretched from Sidney to Wellington to Bombay to rococo Philadelphia. A culture well-symbolized by those Gibbs' style Churches in each place named (Toronto's early Saint James' Cathedral was one, before the fire of 1836).

A culture represented by Frances Brooke's novel, written in 1769, in Quebec City, about British Garrison life there . . . *Emily Montague*—an early *Pride and Prejudice* it is.

A culture reflected in the articulate Diaries and Letters of women such as Ann Langton . . . writing of the trials of a Gentlewoman in Upper Canada, like Mrs. Moodie.

No hayseeds there. But thoughtful, courteous and hard-working gentlefolk who brought their philosophy of neo-platonism, and their politics of Crown-in-Parliament, and their religion of mitigated Catholicism, Anglican . . . to Canada.

This small Hepplewhitish sideboard belongs to the sophisticated English-speaking culture long domiciliated in Canada. With its finely bowed front, its delicate inlays, its oval Adamesque drawer-pulls, its arcaded centre, it is a simplified version of elaborate pieces being made in London by the world's finest craftsmen at the end of the eighteenth century.

You could have found it, in Canada, anywhere from Halifax to Windsor, around 1810. One very similar to it, larger, is at present in Rideau Hall, Ottawa. Both are in that wood distinctive of Eastern North America—Tiger Stripe Maple . . . the poor man's Satinwood!

Wood: maple
Date: about 1810
Place: Canadiana Gallery, Royal Ontario Museum

Adamesque Corner Cupboard

 . . . like some great Iroquois mask, eyes aglint, mouth agape, body half-swallowed by its own mouth, this handsome cupboard comes to you as some phantasmagoric beast—if you see it in terms of its own embodiment and form—and not simply as a period piece. It comes at you strong and solid, broad in the chest, a potency

some Easter Island icon, straddling the land

which is how I see it first. As a being, some personage. Which is how it, he, she, *wants* to be seen. I know, after a dozen years evading this truth.

And this reality acknowledged, why then you are also free to see this godlike statue as a corner cupboard —of a very special kind. In his recent book, *Civilization*, Kenneth Clark talks of "that simple, almost rustic, classicism that stretches right up the eastern seaboard of America, and lasted for one hundred years, producing a body of civilized domestic architecture equal to any in the world."

This cupboard is part of the North American classicism Lord Clark describes. It, along with an intermittent chain of fine houses across southern Ontario, and similar attractive furniture, proves that the fine sensibility of Robert Adam, and his brother James, indirectly touched Upper Canada. This particular piece was probably made about 1810, for one of the numerous Loyalist families who settled in the Kingston area. Variations of it could have been found in such homes as the Alpheus Jones

house, in Prescott, or the Davey house, in Bath.

It is the very expanded, animated, cerebral quality of this cupboard—the inflated frieze, and fan-work, and paterae—which mark this piece for me as North American. Like French Canadian church carvers, the man who created this piece took European high-style elements, and blew them up, larger than life, larger than their own proportions . . . to catch the eye. Hallucinogenic!

And it is the broad beam of it, the very strength and squatness of this cupboard which identifies it for me as Upper Canadian. In contrast with its English cousin, who would be more delicately self-poised; or its Yankee cousin, who would be lighter, less grand.

It has that specific combination of inflated geometric forms (neo-classic), and sheer ponderosity—some almost uneasy balance of mere-mind and sheer-mass, with some additional element of innate elegance, which makes it Yankee-Ontario Loyalist. As though the Loyalists were caught between the stolid virtues of King Billy's Whig Revolution of 1688 and the more purely intellectual assertions of the Age of Enlighten-ment. Plus some tincture of Stuart panache.

This is Ontario: call it . . . High Methodist!

Wood: pine
Date: early 19th century
Place: Canadiana Gallery, Royal Ontario Museum

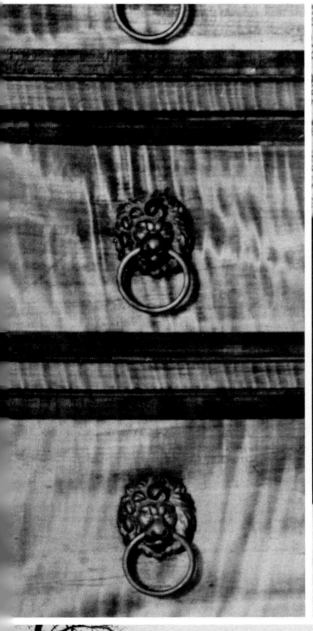

Bureau-Desk

The predicament is clear.

I can touch but do not
I am touchable but untouched
I am in touch but out
Out of touch but in.

And you?—Dear Reader...and you? Are you different from me?
Do you reach out to touch? Are you touched? Or are you too
an untouchable?

It is like the tigerstripe in the early Ontario yeoman furniture.
That ripple there, the curlycue, our virulent sensual compressed
under hard surface of varnish that is steeled veneer. Our
rockbound buried Canadian dapple is this curlymapling.
Victorian corsetted our hearts of Maple struck in that deep wood.

We are the ripple in the tigered maple
constrained in the fleshproof glass.

—these lines throb my head (and my heart)
as I see, once again, this early Ontario Bureau-Desk.
The lines come from the opening chapter of my
novel, *Civic Square*, as I try there-in to place my finger
on the predicament of the Ontario Man: his rising
competence and his declining compassion. And these
are the lines that time and again sum up my feelings,
as I see approach that early Ontario furniture which
is best and most frequently summarized in figured
maple! Some terrible sense of pent-up energy in
such pieces—tables, chairs, chests, beds. A sense of
precisely constrained force—and a very voluptuous
force (look, just gaze in-to that figured maple of this
Bureau-Desk. And as you gaze, somewhere inside,
the lions rroarrr

J. W. McCoubrey, after studying American art, from
early times to the present, developed a simple and
pertinent thesis: that American art (and decor)
tends to fall out, to press beyond, its frame. It is
never contained within its framework—not entirely.

The correlative Canadian thesis is this: that Canadian
arts, especially English Canadian arts, are contained
within a stern system of "peace, order, and good
government." Or said differently—as in Harold Town's
series of paintings—there is always "the tyranny of the
corner!" It is as though Canadians were compressed
within an attractive box...like a Birks' Blue Box, all
tied up with a white ribbon— in Gift—yet unable to
get out. And the question is—how to get out of the
box, how to open the Gift, without either killing
or being killed.

This voluptuous and sumptuous Bureau-Desk, of
Hepplewhite style, which could have been made in
a dozen different towns along the Ontario Front,
prior to 1830...this Bureau-Desk poses our
predicament...beautifully!

Wood: figured maple and pine
Date: about 1820
Place: Canadiana Gallery, Royal Ontario Museum

Loyalist Pembroke Table

...a fine piece of furniture focuses the beauty of a home, a town, a countryside, a people. It becomes some kind of parable, releasing knowledges and insights—the central character in its own novel.

Like this Loyalist Pembroke table, which for me is a trip along the Old Front Road, the King's Highway #2. A trip through Dogwood, rising deep Burgundian red, like arteries up from the sun-breached March snows. And crows drifting across the field furrows, black and proud as Aztec plume-gods... none of the colour birds back yet.

This table a trip to Brockville—with its proud civic square—court house magisterial, and cluster of churches (each one aspiring visually to cathedrality!). Brockville, with its rich agglomeration of High Victorian homes, all gables and towers and laced with verandahs that seem larger than these large houses who are pontificating patriarchs in their own right.

And on beyond Brockville, along the Old Front road—King's Highway #2—the apple orchards turning flesh flush against the remnant snow, beyond grey limestone walls that were standing when the Yankees marched so long age against Crysler's farm near here (they didn't get it).

Ahh—rolling by on my left... stone home, with full wall, stable, side-kitchen, and antique shop. "Stoneacres"—nearly missed it—watching the Saint Lawrence and my soul instead. Back up, and amble into the yard, the child's swing I want to try. But knock instead, apprehensive—maybe they're no longer....

The ruddy laughing face rich with sorrow and knowing comes to the door. And we penetrate the antique shop still toppled full of early Ontario pieces—themselves some kind of collage of our heritage.

"COME ON IN!... the missus will want to see you. Been five years now since." And we wend through the kitchen that is its own "vivoir"—its own room-for-living... laden with vivid ironstone and twinkles of early glass, and—spectating us—a curly-birch spoon rack, the spoons like eyes, heads. Oh—kitchen all cherry and maple and pine and rich as Joe's Rembrandt face.

As we sit and laugh and rock the years off—somewhere just beyond tears, in this scene that is *Jorrock's Jaunts and Jollities*, for real. Spiritually.

"You'll stay for dinner?!" Yes... roast beef and Yorkshire pudding; it's still Sunday. And afterwards, as we adjourn for Port, leaving the simple yet sumptuous dining room, I pass this old table—you are an old friend, svelte and elegant—with your hand-planed cherry top and moulded corners, your finely tapered legs and your arch forms—you, so classically handsome, like this home, and so gently rolling, like the land... and warm to the touch, like our host and hostess.

And I want to bow to you, to you and to a people and a history and to some lost sentimentality, that now we know *was* rooted in reality.

I want to bow... and I do.

Woods: cherry and tiger maple and pine
Date: about 1820
Place: "Stoneacres," home of Mr. and Mrs. Joe
              Flanigan, near Brockville

Painted "Fancy" Chairs

coming down the street, shrill with candied kids, the drums abeating and the bass drum pounding deep. The trumpets in a high brass throat with flutes, piccololalays, and a single trombone—phooomph phooooommphh. The sound all glister and gold like the epaulettes frilling blue-bodied shoulders, and—up front—a Drum Major so glossy and bright he could be a Majorette

THAT'S the feel in this spangle of chairs. The feel of Minute Men, dressed up on parade. The same feel as an imitation Cadillac grill, or an All-American smile, or a football huddle at Playoffs, with confetti and a gaggle of bands, or a neon-ignited shopping Plaza, or a Presidential Convention (all hot-doggerel, and Yankee-doodle-dandle)

and all the crowd starry-eyed and popinjay proud. The Independence Day Parade—permanent July 4: U.S.A.

THAT'S the feel and the sight of this glister of chairs! And that of course is what these chairs are, essentially: a congress of early American painted "fancy" chairs —so popular in improved American homes, from 1810 to 1850 and, via the Boston Rocker, decades later.

These chairs are the frontiers-man-made-good, made gaudy! These chairs are the star-spangled Yankee (all balloons and bauble) in the pride of his new-won Independence. These chairs are Ben Franklin at Versailles, Sam Slick at Buckingham Palace, and a Connecticut Yankee at King Arthur's Court—coonskin couth . . . for Nature's Nobleman!

And their cultural lineage is simple: the eighteenth century elegant English Sheraton chair, passed to the populace with machine mass production

. . . and all gussied up with gilt-paint. Folk Splendour!

But this particular octet of gaudy Yanks has something added. A certain stolidity—is it in the solid front-leg stretcher? Or that massive rope-twist back-stretcher? Or that coronet with ostrich plumes in a visual geyser?

Ahh—that is it—that crown with the Prince of Wales Feathers! Who are at once the heft and the panache of this otherwise garrulous featherweight (Windsor chair on a bank holiday!).

This group of chairs is His Majesty's Yankee! Legitimate descendants of Sir John Johnson's New York Rangers. This is the Upper Canadian Yankee Loyalist—that particular original "American" who, in 1776, and again in the War of 1812, and again with Canadian Confederation in 1867, and again in two World Wars, said clearly who he was and where he stood: the Ontario man—loyal to the Crown and a British form of Democracy . . . a man willing to fight for it!

There is no proof (other than visual!) that these chairs were made in Ontario. But they were probably made at Canadian behest—perhaps as late as 1860—for the visit of the Prince of Wales.

Date: mid 19th century
Place: Cook's Tavern, Upper Canada Village

Teapoy

Canadians have had a hard time accepting themselves! They have been, historically, caught in a North America whose dominant public myth is of a gun-toting Cowboy who shoots his wild way to Heaven and a beautiful woman he rarely kisses. The image of the male is of some brute tamed by bullets. At the same time, within Canada itself, the dominant tradition, over three centuries, is one of Church and Crown. In French Canada—the Catholic Church with its rich pomp. In English Canada—the British Crown with its achievement of "peace, order, and good government"... and its mode of manners (yes—Canada is a novel of manners that will never be written).

The result of this, for Canadians, is a tacit tradition... the tradition that the Canadian Male is a brute mitigated by manners. And if he ever moves beyond civil manners he trips over his own feet. He must not, and can not, be fully civilized! And there is no one that Canadian society respects more and puts down more quickly, than a civilized man.

But the historic evidence is strong in favour of both a civilized Canada and of a Canada that lusted to be civilized. At least the evidence was strong a century and more ago. Far from being a nation of squabbling squatters and dominantly dour Scotch, mid-Victorian Canada shows manifold signs of a concern for delicacy of feeling and of personal presence.

This Teapoy sums up what I am trying to say as well as anything. For the Chinese the Tea Ceremony was a way of being... a ceremony as ritually exact and uplifting as Choral Eucharist. For the English, under Queen Anne, tea resulted in a new form of furniture —the tea table, and in part, a new focal centre to the drawing or living room!—new social finesse found expression in finer furniture... furniture which flowed.

In Canada, the late eighteenth century portrait of Marguerite Mailhot by Beaucourt shows her in full cultural regalia—with her silver tea or coffee pot. While by 1860 the best silverworks for Birks were tea services.

Teapoys, like this, were part of new Victorian plush and prosperity, and the belief that life was *not* merely "nasty, brutish, and short." They could be found in many Canadian homes by the mid nineteenth century.

Woods: cherry and maple
Date: about 1840
Place: Upper Canada Village

Country Dining Table

on the horizon, a cluster of sky-spiked Hemlocks linked to Maple like a fortress. The large barn to one side—and orchard between (buds just beginning so that the trees spurt green)

turn down the long driveway, narrow-eyed, leads straight up up up . . . to a sharp peaked central gable—with jabs of split-rail fence en route

russets speckled (Rhode Island Red, pullet), bright blacks, greys that are green with sun through the clouds . . . stones culled from the fields cleared of those stumps lining the edge of the orchard

Ontario Home—circa 1850: unmistakable, with its particular stance, set square to the land (no nestle), and to the road

overseeing the land, those windows are geometrically placed, glazed eyes stoney-staring straight out at me. So that as I get out of our car I automatically brace my shoulders, straightening myself up before approaching the verandah with its cut-wood trim (Ontario "lace," this verge-boarding

and the particular lilt of bushes, lyric-leaved (gentle ogival) by the house. In six weeks they'll be lush purple (and Hummingbirds). Lilacs

"Oh, Mrs. Schumacher, we've come to see that . . . ."

"Oh yes, it was you that phoned . . . It was made by my great-grandfather, of them Maple trees in the South Twenty. He had eight boys, I've got a photo, the old kind . . . d'ye know!"

as we turn sharp right into the dining room, stop abrupt—held to a standstill by the flare of waving wood; the flame grain criss-crossed by tiger-striping. Rarest of woods. Square yards of it

still standing at attention, almost . . . and slowly relenting (me? or the table?) work my cautious way forward and

"Oh, I'm sorry"—unconscious apology for my fingers stroking the flesh of the wood, responding to the ripple and float beneath gloss of time (less varnishes than accumulation of good spilt gravy, coal-oil, and other human hands)

Mrs. Schumacher just saying "oh, go right ahead" —as though permission to pet her German Shepherd

"It's so aloof at first, and then just drew me in to touch."

We laugh, ice cracked

"They were friendly folk, the Schumachers . . . only got riled once. Grandaddy Ephraim went out to fight in the Uprising in '37"

Wood: figured maple
Date: about 1840
Place: Canadiana Gallery, Royal Ontario Museum

Empire Ontario Sideboard

 Enclosed by full-grown Maple trees and a white-paling fence to stone entry posts. Chestnut trees on the lawn, as large shade-trees. A high white cedar hedge out back, visually blocking the large stable—four-carriage stable!, two stories high with gothic window in the centre of the second story. A stable like some miniature of many full farm houses of the period. In red brick with white-brick quoinings. Like the house itself.

Lilac bushes at the corners of the main house ("Come down to Kew in Lilac time, in Lilac time"). As though Lilacs themselves were some presence of the Old Country, to be found near any Ontario rural home. The seeds sometimes brought with the settlers, the way they brought Hawthorne . . . and the English Sparrow!

The house, as you approach, rising high-browed and robust: full-chested (Diana of Ephesus, almost! Victorian deity). The monolithic lorgnette of that central upper window—Palladian, over the Doric porch; focussing attention to door and house-height, and you.

Truly a Temple! The whole presentation of that straight red-brick (baked on the lot), framed, pillared, at either end by those white brick cornerings. And over the windows those deep eyebrows also white brick.

This is the house that you enter, through the wide doorway with its sidelights and spacious entry hall and walnut-newelled stairway straight-rising . . . wide enough for a couple. Right turn, into the dining room, which has a ceiling as high as the entry hall . . . is it fourteen feet?—with floral plaster mouldings.

Ahh—there he is, at the far end . . . culminate focus of the entire vista that is the house over you. Handsome panorama of Niagara, watercolour, by Whale I suspect, over top. And staunch glass punch bowl—reminding of Waterford. The sideboard an entire Regiment, of County Regulars! Same mass, lines, as the house and lot: upright pilasterings, those end sections, like a single Greek column. And, like the house, piebald—white and red, the whorl of figured golden Maplewood.

Yes, this sideboard, like the house—late Empire, Tuscan Revival, the "glories of Greece and Rome" (towns named after Athens, Sparta, Rome—aspirations after a classic, and imperial, destiny).

Like the man . . . Honest-Ontario-Yeoman-made-good! With both feet solid to the soil.

Half-way between Dundurn Castle, on the one hand, and the American Log-Cabin Myth on the other: this house, this sideboard, this man—all one. The Complete Canadian Cube; the backbone of the State. Been with us now for over a century. We respect and love him . . . almost!

Wood: bird's eye maple
Date: mid 19th century
Place: Canadiana Gallery, Royal Ontario Museum

Ontario Side Table

What is striking about this small, and apparently uninteresting, side-table is its four-square stolidity. It absolutely confronts you—almost affronts you. As though it were saying, quietly, politely, "I'm as good nor you, Mac," an attitude which is in effect only one step removed from that early New England motto: "Don't step on me!" Do you remember that motto?—with the picture of a Rattlesnake coiled back and ready to strike!

Fortunately this piece has less of a death-sting to it, and less a look of New England astringency, than some quality of energy.

Yes—this is what impresses you upon a second look: the charge of kinetic energy. Can you spot where that coiled energy is?

It's turned right in to those stubby, well-muscled legs, and the dark tiger-sharp striping to the Maple wood. That striping nearly has a flagellant quality, again almost, not quite: there is a constraint somewhere.

Add the sharp, firm, cornering to the piece. Almost a "Precision Squad" quality—somewhere there *is* a martinet hidden herein!

In fact, what we have here is the absolute Ontario Fact . . . be it in people, architecture, manners, or furniture. Call it the Complete Cube. That's what this table is: assertively a monolithic cube!

No frills of consequence—but plenty of decor built right in . . . whether turned or curled or coiled. And even where there is a curve, as in the knees of those four legs, the curve is in no way undulant, but unmoving—a straight curve, one might say.

And—this is the decisive thing: the whole thing is buttoned right down—tight! How?—not just in the compactness of the piece . . . but (have you got it?)— that's it: those four drawer handles, dark cherry, which both dress the table up and batten it down!

Aha! That's who. . . .

The man with the neat mustache and the pin-stripe suit.

The Red Ensign!

". . . a place to stand and a place to grow Ontaree-aree-aree-O"

All one and the same thing!

And this table, and variations of it, some more elegant and many much simpler—this table was as common as Collies in early rural and village Ontario.

Wood: tiger maple and walnut
Date: mid 19th century
Place: Canadiana Gallery, Royal Ontario Museum

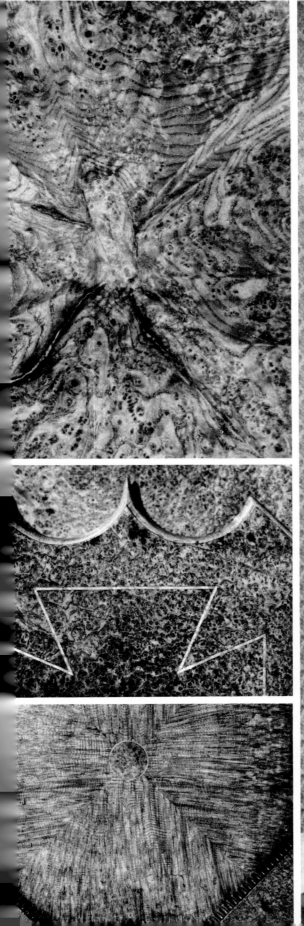

Grandfather Clock

To the untrained eye this Grandfather Clock could pass simply as a provincial piece of a kind perhaps to be found as easily in Upstate New York, Connecticut, rural Pennsylvania, French Canada, or even parts of Ohio, as in Ontario. It would seem rather heavy, even top-heavy. And that is all.

But look more closely!

Firstly, there is the quantity and richness of the grained woods. Even a glance shows half-a-dozen different grains and wood-cuts. Which is unusual, and beautiful, in itself!

Secondly, there is the high equine curve of the broken pediment atop the clock. A kind of flare and depth that is not common in the forms of Anglo-American furniture. At least not after 1750.

And then there is the deep bevelling of the waist, the full-lipped skirt, the strong curve to the top of the door. And, perhaps most striking of all, that fret-cut trim to the sides of the clock top.

Decidedly, there is more to this clock than meets the first detached glance!

Look at it as a man, a person! "Who" is this clock? Is he a New Englander? No—he doesn't have Yankee attenuation. There is no asperity to this clock.

Is he a French Canadian? Noui...!—as the French Canadians would say. Literally "no-and-yes." He has the earthiness of the French Canadian, the large head and the short feet. But he seems at once heavier and less elegant. Surely a French Canadian would have carved something on this piece!

Is he an Upper Canadian? Perhaps. He does have that British Canadian stolidity. Yet in many ways he is too rich, too spicy. He isn't merely an Oxtail Stew man. This is someone who likes Blood Pudding and garlic sausages and tripe. The Honest Ontario Yeoman is too fastidious for this.

Yet it *is* an Ontario piece. It does fit within the Ontario tradition, somehow. The answer is that it is a German-Ontario clock. Of a kind that was not uncommon in the area called Berlin until World War I, and now is named Kitchener-Waterloo. This is a sauerkraut and Bock Beer piece. No need to listen for bagpipes or French horn. This is hefty German folk Baroque. As fully folk Baroque as a small Bavarian Church with onion-dome spires.

That it is folk-German constrained by English culture can be felt in the reduced legs, and some concision to the otherwise lush wood forms.

This particular piece was made in York County, near Markham, about 1840. It still strikes the hour—with sonority!

Wood: walnut, cherry, and maple
Date: about 1840
Place: Canadiana Gallery, Royal Ontario Museum

Tester Bed

 lying abed, toes curled in the flannel sheets, head propped up against the double bolster pillow against the broad, high, staunch bedhead, a single slab of wood reminding me that Canadians were conceived of European oak but now have hearts of maple

the high deep-turned posts, like sculpted marble, and the thickest feet (like hooves), and calves as strong as oxen

overhead the canopy, at once a crown, a frill, and an encasement—and covering me, like spread of Autumn fields...rich, sallow, all pumpkin time and stooks of corn, the pheasant strutting through green black and russet, the twill coverlet

at my left hand, burl candlestand, and wax as soft as honey, fragrant, lit

and blown blueglass washbasin, jug, ripple to my pleased eye on the square bedside table, sturdy, strong and sleek. No nonsense, but much sensuality, in its figured wood

and at my right, the rush-bottom Regency chair, also honey-coloured maple, hand-carved and turned. With the illustrated Old Testament on it; family dates inscribed...marriages, begettings, and "passings on" ("their Memory remaineth sweet to those they left behind")

reassuringly to hand, just beneath the bed, the white porcelain catch-all

and overlooking bed, room, us all, the wide-eyed portrait of a lass...her collie-dog with head raised to the piece of bread she holds aloft (is it bacon-bread, cooked with fine large chunks of lard in it?). And her apple. Some early Ontario Eve

out the window, the high bush cranberry, red flush in the ebbing March snows. And basking between the tongued split-rails, the black cat catches protected sun bask

and a whole world spread on from this bed. The high clapboard house, second home of pioneer Daniel Strong—built in 1832, after sixteen years in his first log home still standing strong beside. The morning sounds of piggery—that friendly reassuring gruntlery that is all intestinally sound. And the chesty mumble of meandering oxen (domiciled Minotaurs). And, just beyond, Roblin's Mill, turning power of river through stone, into fresh flour

I feel at home in this world, that is this bed like some domestic ship of state—calm, firm, sure. In charge of what it sees without need to dominate

and grasping the post I shake the frill overhead. The whole bed quakes bodily. Why...she's as good as a hay ride, Clem!

Wood: figured maple
Date: about 1840
Place: Black Creek Pioneer Village, Toronto

Dundurn Castle Sideboard

 Dovecote on the left, with its host of white spirits (no wonder the Holy Ghost was Dove), the driveway sweeping to monumental portico (remembrance of the Queen, waving, at Buckingham Palace, to a world saved from War.

Daughter Sophia, with that red hair fracturing mere reality, greeting in the front hall—a backdrop of gilt that is instant patina (the console table, was it Lannuier of New York?)

Ushering you in to the glister of cut glass (they said the chandelier has six hundred pieces) and the tinkle of crystals, best Waterford.

Twenty of the county gentry settled for Wild Turkey, roasted with Chestnuts, from the estate.

"Who won in the pit today, Sir Allan?"—having missed the cockfight (wagers were high).

Dinner in Dundurn Castle, Thanksgiving, 1847. Ten years since the ragamuffin Mackenzie upset public order with his baby rebellion. A toast to that and to "Sir Allan Napier MacNab—the strong right arm of the British Crown." Echoing the Duke of Wellington's phrase of praise.

"More wine!"—the MacNab laughs, and the Head Butler (who doubles as head gardener) recedes to the sideboard, and raises the left pediment of the same, bringing forth two magnums of Burgundy Red.

The sideboard presiding behind Sir Allan as some dais. Massive in deep bevelled walnut cut from the Hamilton Mountain, and following the latest Tuscan Villa architecture as befits this Canadian Castle. Yes— the first of its kind in North America, the culture of the Crown taking the lead in Canada once again. Democracy ain't civilized!

"I want a house fit for Royalty to visit," the Laird said. It was ... leaving Sir Allan deeply in debt, even though he did run the Grand Trunk Railway right through his own backyard overlooking Lake Ontario. And even though he did go on to become Prime Minister of both the Canadas—Upper and Lower.

Sir Allan is long gone, and Canada no longer tolerates baronets (Mackenzie's ghosts saw to that in post-humous revenge). But Dundurn remains, some baby-Blenheim Palace—more elegant than ever, open to the public. Sophia's Diaries are still there. And beside Sir Allan's chair at the head of the table, stands his gout stool (too much wine?). While this pedimented sideboard, built right into the arcaded end wall does duty for the MacNab.

Wood: walnut
Date: about 1845
Place: Dundurn Castle, Hamilton

Aunt Sophia's Sitting Room

 1860. The eye moved vertically instead of horizontally. Gables, dormers, verandahs, spires, decorative trim—all conspired to lift the eye up, and to frill it. North America had gone Gothic!

Alexander Jackson Downing had dotted the United States countryside with Gothic Revival villas. In Canada the change was even more decisive: Gothic—following the British Mother of Parliaments, rebuilt in the 1840's—was quasi-official. It captured the Canadian Parliament, of course, and even the squat Methodist mind of Toronto. The Anglican Church in Canada built such monuments as Saint James in Toronto or—even more Puginesque, and designed in part by Butterfield himself—the Cathedral in Fredericton.

It was the age of the *Apologia pro vita sua* . . . the Anglo-Catholic revival in England. And a revitalization of the Monastic life. Queen Victoria herself was about to enter a life of model Christian mourning for the dead Prince: and the Albert Memorial would be a miniature Gothic Cathedral!

The prevalent Ontario farmhouse of today was built then—with its high-pinched front gable and its neo-Gothic lacery. Elizabeth Cottage in Kingston is but an elaborate and delicate variation of the theme. The Ontario yeoman aspired to Manners and to a solid decorum.

Here, in Aunt Sophia's Room in Dundurn Castle, we can see Canada at the moment of transition—in the mid 1840's. The room itself is still a solid square—a heavy "British" square. But the corner is cut and the windows are heavily curtained in visual plush and the curtain-cornices are repoussé crowns, while banners surmount the Gothic mantle—frilled heat-screens—and ferns are part of the natural order of things. To the left, the occasional table is a heavy maple Ontario chunk, but its skirt moulding is original. And the central table is round, the sofa undulates earnestly, and—to the right—the fine tiger-stripe maple Secretary Bookcase has a deeply bevelled front-panel and (the finger of the immediate future) Gothic tracery in the windows of the doors. Many rooms in Ontario, Québec and the Maritimes resembled this one by the time of Confederation . . . a frilled square.

The United States built the Enlightenment on top of the Middle Ages—but Canada tried to rebuild the Middle Ages on top of the Age of Reason. The overall result is unmistakable.

Wood: figured maple
Date: about 1845
Place: Dundurn Castle, Hamilton

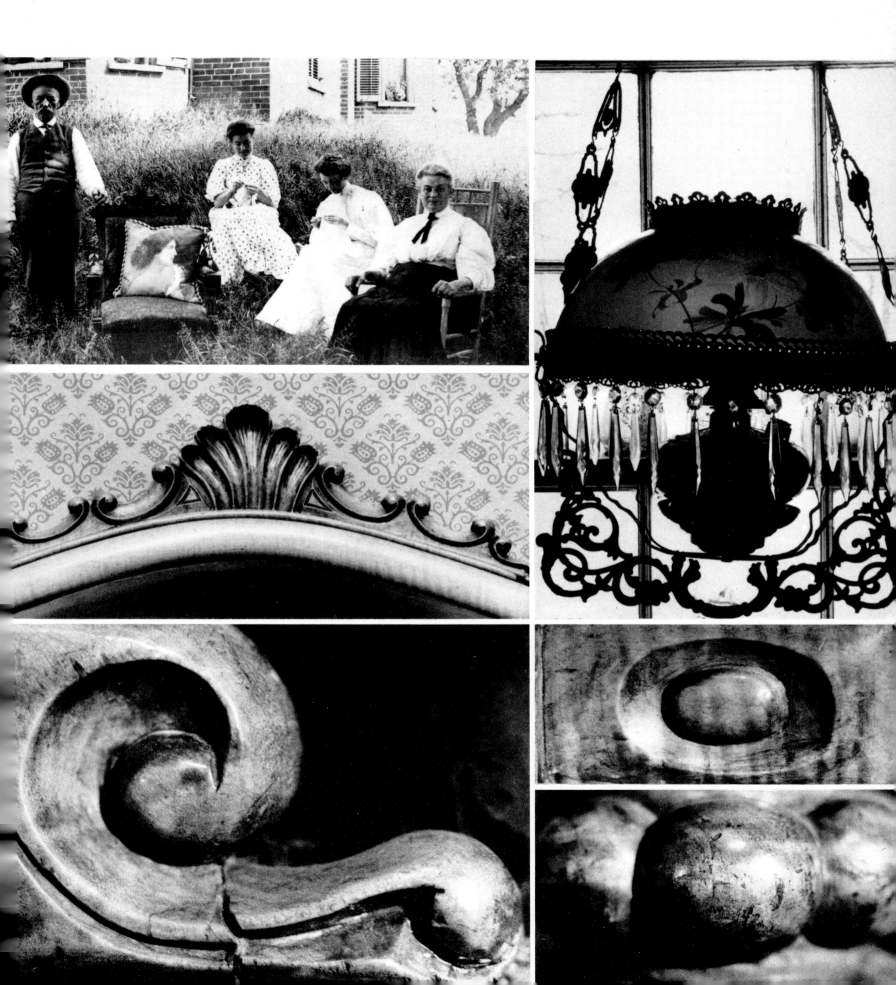

Victorian Sofa

 A massive and blood-red elegance, which beckons—but, even as you approach, something about this sofa stands you off. Far from thinking of sitting on it, you find yourself stiffening up in respectful response —eyeing it as it eyes you. There is a moment of mutual appraisal.

And while you are standing there at semi-attention, standing to bidden attentiveness, you may note the firm undulance of the skirt, and the poised arms, and the arched back—an overall visual flow to the piece. And the strong striping of the golden maple. Yes, it all flows—and yet: take a second look.

It doesn't really flow at all. Now that you look directly at it—it only seems to have flowed out of the first wink of your cornered eye. No—it is static and straight, like that line across the bow of the skirt. In fact, this sofa squares *you* off! And you realize that any undulance in it is the opposite to spontaneous . . . merely contained within the mindful eye: hers, and yours!

All of this in a few seconds: the experience of the sofa somehow pulling you together, rendering you more dense, densifying you.

Then you move forward again. After all, it's only a sofa! But you feel a concern: "NOW JUST SIT DOWN PROPERLY"—that's what she says.

"No, Ma'am, I *never* sprawl, much less . . . NO MA'AM! I didn't even think *that*!"

And, somewhere, echoing in the back of your mind, the phrase "WE ARE NOT AMUSED." And you remember the Fleet, all those Ironclads and Dreadnoughts, and the Empire upon which The Sun Never Set. (Even the sun never dared set in Her presence.) And you know whom you are sitting . . . not on, WITH, IN THE PRESENCE OF . . . yes, it's the Victorian Matriarch in all her dignitarianism, and armed to the teeth with interlocking vetoes. She *is* the Dreadnought, the Ironclad.

What is interesting about this sofa, once you are released from visual allegiance by feeling your way through to Who she is—what is interesting is the contrast between Victorian Rococo and eighteenth century French Rococo. The French style is infinitely more lyrical, asymmetrical, light and delicate—truly flowing, truly organic. Whereas this Victorian piece is immobile—finally, she can't move. She is truly an Ironclad. And you know she uses her decor to reign, to rule . . . whereas French Rococo flows to seduce. The Victorian Queen is a dictator; the French decor a delight!

There can be little question that this Dreadnought issues from some small-town Ontario home. Oh yes, I admire her and feel some warmth hidden in the grain. But she'd be fiendish to live with unless you wanted to submit to her, and I didn't!

Wood: figured maple
Date: about 1850
Place: Canadiana Gallery, Royal Ontario Museum

Courthouse Bench-Desk

When I first saw this remarkable oval bench-that-is-also a desk—I was fascinated and delighted. It was such a simple, rich, self-contained piece—like a boat. And the chocolate of the walnut is as satisfying as chocolate always is!

I stopped short, to look—admiring the stability, the obvious practicality (I did not know what it was for!), and the couthness of it. Only then did I notice the label—which told me that this is a desk-cum-bench from an Ontario Courthouse. Which instantly made sense—this piece has all the certitude, even the stateliness of the courthouse. And I remembered, in my mind's eye, that string of old (and new) Court Houses from Windsor to Halifax. The more I looked at this bench-desk the more I saw those Court Houses. Until I realized that in English Canada, certainly, the Court House is a more important visual land-mark than the Churches are! Perhaps this is because there is no single Church in English Canada...but always a denominational cluster of Churches, spread about the town. There are no real "cathedrals" in English Canada. But the Court House was for everyone in a town. And it was large, even pretentious—smacking of every ounce of dignity and high justice that it could. While, in Québec, the Court House, second to the Church, is called a "Palais de Justice"—a *Palace* of Justice.

The small County Court House, in Saint Andrews.

New Brunswick, with its oversized carved Royal Coat of Arms; the massive brute of a Palais, in Québec City; the fine stone Court House in Brockville...or the mod-monumental new Court House in Toronto, lending dignity to the New City Hall. And, summing them all up—that Court House in Cobourg—of the 1850's. A small town of a few thousand building a "palace" to rival Toronto's Saint Lawrence Hall in elegance. A building fit for the Prince of Wales to open!

The United States was primarily dedicated to "life, liberty and the pursuit of happiness." But Canada, in its Confederal British North America Act of 1867, stressed "peace, order and good government"! Justice and order were more important to British Canadians, and beleaguered French Canadians, than any highfalutin' idea of anarchy.

This Courthouse piece reminds me of all of this. And tells me of all of this. It sums up a quality of so many Victorian Canadian homes—foursquare, stolidity (the Britishness in Canadianity). And I note that even while this desk is round (oval), and richly padded: it feels square and thick and un-moving, like the mid-Victorian Ontario farmhouse.

Wood: walnut
Date: about 1860
Place: Canadiana Gallery, Royal Ontario Museum

Carved Maple Walking Cane

I have walked with you

Under the willow planted as shoots by my father

along our driveway where the Kestrel nested. Willow, not weeping, as I often wished I could, but fresh apricot-coloured along the dropping branchlets of first April sap

I have walked with you by the cattail swamp where the Sora Rail whinnied (we had muskrats that Spring, but I wanted to call them Swamp Beaver: it seemed more dignified)

I have walked with you (the earth to hand) past the Mountain Ash we brought in for the Cedar Waxwings, and the Honeysuckle cluster at the hill edge overlooking black tarmack too close for silence (and the sibilances of sun-struck Meadow Larks (we hid in the corn

I have walked with you, down by the river—Duffins Creek—when the Fiddleheads sprung (frying pan fresh) and the Ovenbird sang and I knew I could push on, to seek Morel—yes—just beyond, where the Yellow Orchids swarmed together (those that weren't first eaten by the rabbits, who like Orchids as much as me

And I have walked joy-bidden with you, under the pine, needles sprung to my barefeet. That day we saw—you and me—in the flowering cherry a breech of blue and white flash I knew oh just knew was Black Throated Blue. It could have been the Second Coming

I have walked with you along our lane, mush loam underfoot (Marigolds clenched as good as fresh capers). And heard Thrush shatteringly nearby—

which one? I never saw but just the song like a golden fern rising

I have walked with you our concession side-road round, stopping to admire the stone foundation of Joe Emp's barn (landmark itself—both Joe and barn, I loved . . . terribly (but never told him, dead now

Oh, I've been with you in Trillium Spring, Golden Rod Summer, and Purple Astered Autumn when (do you remember? please!) that Red Tailed Hawk we saw was all the land in flight to a blue-bird sky over Osler's Bluff

And, yes, I've walked with thee in Winter. People thought I was mad . . . when the ice blew dry across the stinging snow. But I wore a ceinture flêchée, and laughed. And watched for Buntings . . . and a cup of tea, at Dick Day's

Yes—I've walked with thee ever since we met. In an Antique Fair, you were lying all casual, under a thick-plank Harvest Table. I bought you for fifteen dollars—dignitarian in your Tigered Maple, your imitation Hawthorne knots, and your long snakes chasing those poor frogs. I wondered—did the man who made you hail from Tipperary, Armagh, like my grandmother's folks, half-a-civilization ago? I do not know

But we have walked together . . . thee and me, all Ontario in hand. In some kind of blessing. And I want—too late!—to thank thee.

Wood: curly maple
Date: about 1860
Place: in private hands

"And the sum and source of all quickness, we will call God.
And the sum and total of all deadness we may call human.
And if one tries to find out wherein the quickness of the
quick lies, it is in a certain weird relationship between that
which is quick and—I don't know; perhaps all the rest of
things. It seems to consist in an odd sort of fluid, changing,
grotesque or beautiful relatedness. That silly iron stove
somehow *belongs*. Whereas this thin-shanked table doesn't
belong. It is a mere disconnected lump, like a cut-off finger."

D. H. Lawrence, in his essay on "The Novel."

Ave atque vale . . . .

...with a twenty-foot house-trailer, to live close to land, the houses, the people...to hug these close. Starting out in the South-Western tip of Ontario—Point Pelee National Park, in early May. Watching the Trilliums and Warblers sprouting Spring (each time a warbler touched a branch tip it burst green!).

Trips into the surrounding countryside—spotting those mid nineteenth century Ontario farmhouses, red-and-white brick. Getting my eye in. And, on Sundays, ending up at the local Anglican Church—instinctively steeping in that "beauty of holiness" that is our age-old faith.

Then in June, my eye attuned to land and homes, setting out—to follow Spring and Summer across Eastern Canada—till Autumn bled the harvests home again.

Along the old #3 Highway, Blenheim, Rodney (historic names in British history), past Port Talbot where Colonel Talbot's early log manor still stands. And as I drive, realizing that something is watching me. Uneasily aware of being stared at. Which I cannot understand. Till I catch their eye—ahh, the wide-eyed windows, the high-chested fronts, the sternly laced verandahs: the Ontario farmhouses; Victoriana, *watching* me! Strong, sturdy, straddling the land—commandeering my admiration, yet at the same time holding me off at arm's length. Some yeoman version of Holbein's Henry VIII, these homes. Uncrowned majesty...somehow.

St. Thomas, focussing the reality of this definitive Victorian Ontario farm home. Because St. Thomas is simply an agglomerate of these farm houses grown bigger and more ornate, and stuck together. Contiguous—but not really touching.

Aylmer, Simcoe, Chippewa, where my folk were first buried on the Canadian side of the water, the Niagara water—nearly two centuries ago now. And the Niagara River, with turbulent majesty. Knowing that this waterway may be the real divide between historic Canada and the United States. If Niagara Falls and gorge had not existed, then Americans would have moved on into indefensible Ontario lands—back in 1800, 1812.

And the Niagara Parkway, all peace and green and quiet, with Brock's monument standing high over the gorge. A hero if we ever had one.

Queenston landing, where family legend said that Simcoe's gunboat brought my people over to the British side. Queenston, with its quiet homes and lanes, like some English village. Or some equally lost eighteenth century American village! And I want to get lost here . . . again. And up to my left, through the skyhigh pines, the majestic Roman architecture of Willowbank—some permanent metaphor out of "Gone with the Wind"; remembering me that the Cavalier tradition came North, after the American Revolution.

Niagara-on-the-Lake—some live dream from our immediate and ever past—with its Palladian Gothic Church. And its main street that can only be strolled. Breakfast at the Oban Inn, overlooking Ontario's lake! With time for tea and marmalade. Sinking in to the monumentally comfortable Victorian sofas.

The back road, gravelled, around Saint Catharine's, through Jordan, with its old stone homes, its fine Church on the hill, up inside it, to admire the weaving on the prayer cushions, the altar frontal. And to pray awhile.

Ball's Falls—jack-in-the-pulpit everywhere.

Dundas, with its greystone homes, and its resident sage, George Grant, in his red-and-white-brick "century Ontario home". . . screened by chestnut trees and tulips. A centre of peace. Explaining to him what I hope to do . . . to see, to *be* on this voyage in to the old, original Canadian culture, once more. Call it a "sentimental journey" . . . to set my heart at ease. "Yes *yes*, DO it Scott . . . *hurry* and do it," George says.

Hamilton, where my mother's mother's family sat in Presbyterian fief—a century ago. Stern, handsome men and women they were. Like Paul Peel's portraits said. County versions of the High Society Henry James depicted in Boston, London.

And on to Dundurn Castle, which reminds me that Casa Loma has roots in Upper Canada.

Burlington, where my father's family received their Crown Grant of Land, as Loyalists. The original home still standing up to five years ago, when it was burnt, to clear the land for a public park. I asked the authorities if they could not keep the home, as a restaurant and utility. And I stayed, for the auto da fé!

The Queen Elizabeth Way, to Toronto, past huge

Ford factories belching fire and finance. Port Credit—Mazo de la Roche land. Oh, she too was a romantic. But now her dream is gone, and seems all the more real. Canadians are, after all, simply romantics who lost the courage of their hopes.

Metropolitan Toronto, engulfing my truck and trailer home. Four, six, ten, twelve lanes. Am I proud of such size, or simply afraid?

Toronto the Good, City of Churches they named it, in my grandfather's era. All I can see are bank towers and trust companies now.

And the old Parliament buildings, Queen Vic asquatting—with the business palaces dependant from her very lap, down University Avenue.

Everything here solid, stolid, foursquare—unbending! All one and the same thing. Things which touch but do not marry.

And as I leave Toronto there is something heavy in me—which is maybe the very weight of the city itself. Its very density and solidity. Moving off the speedway onto the Old Front Road—Highway #2. To Port Hope—which is the first complete old Ontario town east of Toronto. With its half-dozen sharp spires, a prickly agglomerate of faiths, all protesting. And its red-brick mainstreet—so uprighteous.

And in the morning, saluting the Bluestone House as I leave . . . to Cobourg, with its mastodon Court House—some lost British palace standing firm in the midst of this nineteenth century Ontario town. The core of justice—again unbending, stolid—dispensing a truth as immitigable as the Ontario brick farmhouses.

Cobourg—and some miles on, that delicate white clapboard presence who is the Barnum House. Stopping to pay homage to this Greek Revival beauty settled here on the Ontario Front. Yankee dash at its most delicate. Just as the Cobourg Court House was British majesty at its mightiest. Here on the old frontier. Both of them ancestors-in-common. Ours.

Taking lair in Prince Edward County—a kind of private rural keep, slung low into Lake Ontario—at Ameliasburgh. And walking the country roads, see standing against the horizon, a massive farm home—at once cottage blown large, and castle writ small—some baby Blenheim this. And as I approach, realize what it is. Simply the most rotund mutation of the Honest

Ontario farmhouse I have yet seen. It brings together the early rectangular and simple building (is it log underneath?) that was first home, as an outbuilding in the back; plus the gothic Victorian farmhouse with its peaked front gable (like some affronted lorgnette!); plus the High Victorian cube-shaped bulked house, added on front. All of these, partly grown out of each other, partly added on to each other—partly organic and partly mindful—all of these brought together as a single home! The absolute nineteenth century Ontario farm home. Red-and-white brick . . . and all the elements bound together by a fully foliating verandah, which starts at the old back door (the gothic middle house) and comes right round the front to embrace the main block of the newer house . . . culminating in a fine bay window through which I see a mass of plants in pots.

And inside are richly grain-painted cupboards and woodwork; pine, hand-painted to look like golden oak, mahogany and walnut. Full of swoop and flare. And upstairs, matching suites of monumental bed, dressers, wash-stand. With flowering violets in the windows. And—in the upstairs front hall, Victorian tassellated chairs, as deep and as square as the house itself. I walk out on to the second story verandah . . . commanding a view of Roblin's lake and all the valley. Then down the front stairs, with its walnut bannister and at the foot, upright, thickset, with squared shoulders and a rounded knop—the newel post grasps my hand.

As I leave, walking down the snake-railed road, I am saying over and over to the song of the crescent-breasted Meadowlarks, "this is the ancestral roof, this is the ancestral roof—mine and thine. This is the very flesh of a people, the way they walk, stand, talk—solidly, fully. Eyes straight ahead. No fooling . . . Ontario—Ontaree-aree-areeoh."

And as I walk, I spot one, two, several of these homes—variations of each other, around the horizon.

Next day, picking up some homemade pumpkin (and gin!) jam . . . and moving on:

Kingston, with its munificence of garrison greystone and Ganonoque, a rural mutation of Kingston and Bath, an elegant diminutive of Ganonoque to Upper Canada Village, where all of old Ontario lies to hand, our past as a manageable visual metaphor.

This was my voyage through old Ontario—not as breathless as seems. Yet every time I stopped, there was something about Ontario itself—the cumulative culture of it, all round me—which firmly kept me at once standing up and moving forward! As though this was the secret of Ontario civilization—and its very success!

*　*　*

At Cornwall I notice a decisive change.

The West side of the town is very respectable twentieth century Victorianate. But as I move Eastwards through it, the houses become less stern, the neon signs seem gaudier. And the names on the storefronts are French! For the next fifty miles, literally before my very eyes, I watch this remarkable visual metamorphosis: Ontario-into-Québec. British Upper Canada becoming la Nouvelle France . . . No longer are the homes marching in rectilinear dialogue with the highway. But gradually they crowd in on one another—in a friendly garrulous higgledy-pigglement. Even the wood trim on the homes perceptibly changes, from a kind of wooden symmetry to something more akin to actual lace. By the time that I am twenty-five miles on into French Canada I am aware of what has happened. The British square, that rectitudinous cube (in stone or brick) that is old Ontario, has been breached—the body is beginning to undulate, from within! And I note that I am no longer driving by the line in the centre of the road—but instead from the homes or trees or buildings on each side. . . .

Ducking quickly through Montréal—because now it is hot July (and I have spent all Winter researching in Montréal)—with time only to enjoy the flowers sprouting all over in le Vieux Quartier (my God—it's Paris, with its kiosques and flea-markets and lounging lovers!)—on along the North Shore of the Saint Lawrence. Evading neon-lights and tourist gimcrap. Till beyond Trois Rivières, the road crosses a bridge— phoooosh—right into the lap of the Church of Sainte-Anne-de-la-Pérade, this dollshouse "cathedral" which is some echo of Notre Dame in Montréal.

Deschambault—where the river banks rise high over the Sainted Lawrence, and Thomas Baillargé's glorious twin-towered church stands—*not* right-angular to either road or river, but at once set in, and riding high from, the accepting land. A majesty. Marrying river and Tiger Lilies in profusion, and fieldstone, and village. All unified in this single centre of praise. Yes . . . we *can* be saved!

And with this O altitudo in my heart, settle deeper in my driving seat, and start the slow process of slowing down. In Québec there is Time still—and Time is not something to beat—but something to celebrate.

I camped outside Québec City, on the Ile d'Orleans, in a small private park—amidst the glittering Birch trees. Not seeing the Saint Lawrence, yet feeling it— in the eddying silences. And in the morning I drove down to Saint François, walking among the deep brown cattle, who—I suddenly saw—were the live, animal, forms of Québec chests-of-drawers. The land and the animals in the eye of the craftsman. To the church beside the river, and feeling peace and giving thanks.

Hunting the quarry in Québec City for a few days . . . finding ample—the splendrous Baroque Bed, whose very body sums up the trip from Cornwall to la Ville de Québec herself. The very way it moved. And Saint Michael slaying his friendly dragon (Catholic evil seems more graceful than Protestant).

But it was the Ile d'Orleans itself which was spiritual home. Visiting old friends, artists, farmers, judges—all living side to side, in the old homes. Seeing Jean-Charles Bonenfant, mowing his lawn . . . stopping to chat, as always. "You are living an Odyssey . . . back to your roots," he said. "Yes . . . before they are gone," I replied.

And an evening on the East side of the island, at the home of Benoit Côté, the painter . . . an eighteenth century farmhouse which he had made into his studio. Overlooking the Saint Lawrence, with the Falls of Montmorenci in the dusk distance, and the shimmer of lights from Québec City, twenty miles down to our left. Quel Bec! We sat amidst the deep Asters, and drank Chateauneuf du Pape while his bear-sized dog (un Bouvier de Flandre) romped.

Leaving Québec with sadness. Toronto is our Great City, our mod-Methodist New York. And Montréal is our gay city, our Paris. But Québec, ahh (I admit it happily) Québec is our Eternal City!

At Montmagny, stopped short, by a presence so unlike

Québec—either land or people or homes. A great nineteenth century blockhouse of a building. The *form* of an Ontario brick yeoman home. But greystone —British. The British Canadian presence here, in some alien and handsome majesty. I went up—curious . . . the Hôtel des Érables it is now—for dinner, which was substantial and good.

Staying at a small French Canadian trailer park, at Lac-Trois Saumons—Chez Ti-Bert. In the world of Kreighoff-for-real. Psychedelic gypsies, these old French Canadian folk. Hippies with Real Presence!

I meant to stay only a night—but I stayed three, four . . . near the flowers and the tame ducks, and Ti-Bert himself walking as though in some perpetual square-dance that was far from square.

And on Sunday going to the Mass at Saint-Jean-Port-Joli, remembering that this was the parish that had a solid gold Communion Service made at the end of the eighteenth century—by Ranvoyzé, I think. These poor peasants marooned in a Canadian Winter—giving thanks . . . and a gold chalice.

And that afternoon I moved on, deeper into my Trek, finding signs of life and being. Following the dirt-and-gravelled roads. Amazed at the farms. Amidst rock and islands of good soil, their setting was tougher than Ontario—yet the homes were more lyrical. The verandahs more ornate. And always a rocking chair . . . and someone in it.

Moving from St-Alexandre some fifty miles to the New Brunswick border, and then another fifty miles within New Brunswick to Edmunston, a strange event occurred. The French Canadian church metamorphosed before my very eyes. Those splendid grand-yet-simple stone parish churches lost some elegance, some life-slung quality—and became at once heavier and somehow more ornate. The stonework became sterner, less rhythmic. And in Edmunston, the Catholic Church was a huge, heavy stone monument. I had witnessed the passage from la Nouvelle France, to Catholicism within English-speaking Canada. Actually Edmunston is the capital of the Acadian French. And what I was seeing was the Canadian French adapting the very body of their belief to English-speaking eyes.

Something else occurred. I was not only passing from Catholicism to Protestantism. I was also passing along the U.S. border. Not two, but three cultures were

mingle-mangling. On my right, across the St. John River, the stark white farm homes, all rectilinearity, and almost paperweight—in contrast with Ontario rectitudinosity. And in contrast with the enlivened substance of French Canadian homes, these white clapboard facades felt like movie-sets. It was New England, northern Maine, jutting up into the very joints of Canada. And in general contrast with these New England homes, New Brunswick farms were somewhat heavier. It was a precise example of three faiths, expressed in three different forms, fighting to claim the land.

A day and a night at a camp called Mountain View, looking up to Blue Bell Mountain—a sweet symmetry! Talking with the neighbouring farmer . . . and going for dinner—on blue Scandinavian china—with home-made Aquavit. I was in the heart of an old Danish settlement. So I stayed another day, and then two, three. Going to the small white wooden church atop the hill nearby. The valley and hills rolling out beyond, like Devonshire. The church was Danish Lutheran . . . and inside, the wall-panelling was that feathering I recognized from Scandinavian country homes. The pastor invited me for lunch.

When I left, a week later, I had Ontario in my bones, French Canada in my soul, and New Brunswick in my blood!

At Fredericton I knew a professor of Canadian History, Ken Windsor. And I ended up giving a "lecture" to his students—in comparative visual geography: the grid-iron flattened manscape of old Southern Ontario compared with the rumpling and rising Saint Lawrence Magnificat of Québec, and now the rolling hills and rivers of New Brunswick. How the houses were the people, were the furniture and the churches and the sounds of the voices. How Ontario voices came from without, like memos, as external affairs; and Québec voices were nasal and internal—like their deep little homes, and in New Brunswick it was a bit of both.

And later Ken and I talked of what I was *really* doing: this personal Odyssey in-to the heart of early Canadian belief . . . with furniture as central evidence of an entire culture. Ken was thrilled—and said "you know —we forget how much religion was the core of early Canadian life." So I opened up and explained that in our early furniture I found the evidence of all this. How the stolid sentience of Ontario furniture, the uncompromising and straight mass of it, was the same as the early Ontario homes and people. And how these were the same as the early Presbyterian and Methodist brick and stoney churches. How—when all was said and done—Ontariana was Methodism with improved manners. High Methodist. A world of extrinsic emotions!

Ken laughed, and offered me a glass of Hoch—so I vouchsafed the Québec correlative: the tumescent Saint Lawrence land, austere, yet sumptuous, like the churches, like the Armchair à la Canadienne, or the Saint-Geneviève commodes, like Sir Wilfrid Laurier . . . the inner fleshed rythms of these, a total human presence—that becomes, in the Mass, the total Presence of Christ . . . Body and Blood. So that I understood the Medieval experience of Blood running down the Altar.

And now, in the Maritimes, something else again—something "other." Oh, something in between. Some of the cubicular form of Ontario—but lighter. With some flow. Ontario is stone and brick and stolidity. The Maritimes are wood and winds. "And water," said Ken. And there is some of that inner music that is Québec; sounds are intrinsic. "The Maritimes are 'folk Whig,'" Ken offered—"the Real Presence is there if you want it."

Next morning we walked down from the University Campus . . . along that street of munificent Victorian wooden homes, where Bliss Carmen and Charles Roberts spent some mutual youth. To Morning Song in the Anglican Cathedral. We were the only ones there.

Thence I drove to Gagetown, where Sir Leonard Tilley was born . . . visited his childhood home—so simple and elegant. Gagetown—where the Black Watch recently held their final parade. And grown men wept.

And on, to Saint John, Sackville, Halifax—always questing . . . and the evidence growing—of our past, the reality of the furniture as the flesh and faith of our peoples. One and the same.

So that by August I was in Port aux Basques, Newfoundland. Resting for a week in the small fishing outport of Trout River. And staying five months!—assimilating all that I had seeing been. Till in January I reached Saint John's. And here I found a large version

of what I had already seen in Trout River. A people and a culture as old as the Tudors, living in homes that were some fluent folk combination of medieval substance and Georgian lines. Medieval fidelity and Georgian lucidity. And—like the Mallard House at Quidi Vidi—possessed of furniture ranging in style from the Iron Age through to Victorian blown silvered glass candlesticks. Everything had been kept, everything had grown.

And when I left Saint John's a few weeks later my body and my mind and soul were at one. I wanted to sing . . . I had followed the forms of our past clean across Eastern Canada—living close to them, living in them—for over a year. I had sought and found our hidden or forgotten ancestors. And I knew for certain that the furniture of the old homes was equally the furniture of the heart and mind and soul of these people. The forms of one were the forms of all the rest. Yes, I had tracked the ancient forms of our faith, from the heart of a great continent, to where they began, at the bitten edge of land and ocean. And at the very moment when it was clear that my people had to make their ultimate choice, between faith and cynicism . . . I had renewed my faith—and I rejoiced. . . .

Bibliography

American:

Downs, Joseph. *American Furniture:
Queen Anne and Chippendale Periods
in the Henry Francis du Pont Winterthur Museum.*
N.Y.: Macmillan, 1952.

Comstock, Helen. *American Furniture:
A Complete Guide to Seventeenth, Eighteenth
and Nineteenth Century Styles.*
N.Y.: Viking, 1962.

Kovel, Ralph & Terry. *American Country
Furniture, 1780-1875.*
N.Y.: Crown, 1965.

Montgomery, Charles F. *American Furniture of
the Federal Period 1788-1825.*
N.Y.: Viking, 1966.

Ormsbee, Thomas H. *Field Guide to Early
American Furniture.*
Boston: Little, Brown, 1951.
Also in paperback.

_____ *Field Guide to American
Victorian Furniture.*
Boston: Little, Brown, 1952.
Also in paperback.

Otto, Celia Jackson. *American Furniture of
the Nineteenth Century.*
N.Y.: Viking, 1965.

Williams, Henry L. *Country Furniture of
Early America.*
N.Y.: A. S. Barnes, 1963.

Canadian:

MacLaren, George. *Antique Furniture by
Nova Scotia Craftsmen.*
Toronto: Ryerson, 1961.

Minhinnick, Jeanne. *Early Furniture in
Upper Canada Village, 1800-1837.*
Toronto: Ryerson, 1964. Paperback.

Palardy, Jean. *The Early Furniture of
French Canada.*
Toronto: Macmillan, 1965.

Ryder, Huia. *Antique Furniture by New
Brunswick Craftsmen.*
Toronto: Ryerson, 1965.

Stevens, Gerald. *Early Ontario Furniture.*
Toronto: U. of T. Press, 1966.
Paperback.

Stewart, Don. *A Guide to Pre-Confederation
Furniture in Upper Canada.*
Toronto: Longmans, 1967.

Note in thanks

In the two years that I have been working full time on this book, and during the ten years which I spent visiting private and public collections of furniture throughout Eastern North America, I was only once turned away from a door—by a very attractive lady who (probably quite rightly) disliked one of my novels. It can be asserted with assurance that hospitality among connoisseurs is warm and sustaining.

Explicitly, this book would not have been possible without the ample friendship of George Spendlove, former Curator of Canadiana at the Royal Ontario Museum. And of Dr. E. P. Richardson, one-time Director of the Henry Francis du Pont Winterthur Museum. For each of these men the study of furniture and of decor was also a spiritual meditation.

As a one-time curator of Canadiana, I spent many hours with antique dealers across Canada. Laughing and gossiping (pungently) and touching the objects with afficionados as various as Bert Baron, Sonny Booth, Sam Breitman, Herbert Schwarz, John Russell and Gerry Brenner, Mogens and Margaret Philip, and Les Donaldson. We were of all ages and genders and creeds. But whenever a piece of fine Canadiana was forthcoming, we were bound as comrades-in-arms for ever. There was much joy.

So too those private citizens who are badly named "collectors." They, we, are really acolytes in some apparently arcane but really very simple religion: an incarnate knowledge of God and of Grace—by whatever name you choose—through the object. I think happily of evenings and of excursions, with Stella and John Langdon, Paul LaCroix, Benoit Cote, Charlie de Volpi, Barbara Richardson, Peter Winkworth, Paul Godfrey, Helen Ignatieff and June Biggar. To name only a few.

Together we "travelled in realms of gold." And I would like to confess now what I never dared—that I loved our hours together much much more than any Wasp should! Indeed, I now know that these hours together, cumulatively saved me from Waspdom.

Over the years as I lived with, felt, and fondled fine furniture, I came increasingly to recognize that objects embodied a spiritual reality of potence. Two men went far out of their way to help me admit this—and thus started my spiritual Odyssey. Gabriel

Marcel, the Christian existentialist, and Charles Moeller, now Rector of the Oecumenical Institute in Jerusalem. They are often in my prayers.

As a child I was often dragooned into travelling the countryside with my immeasureable grandfather, William Perkins Bull ("W.P.")—gathering data for his historical series on beloved Peel County. I learnt my field work young—and not without chagrin!

My father, Harry Symons, imbued me with a gentle love of trees and wildflowers and birds and finally old fences. Because of him my knowledge of Canadiana could never become merely academic.

During World War II, when household help dis-appeared overseas, my mother used her large brood to keep our lovely home clean—polishing, dusting, waxing, exquisite furniture, mahogany panelling, eighteenth century silver. Intimate touch with beautiful objets d'art: this was my *real* education!

In the final writing of this book, a friend and colleague, John McConnell, and I travelled across Eastern Canada, from Windsor, Ontario, to Saint John's Newfoundland—in a truck, camper, and trailer: our land-boat. During this year-long "furniture safari" many people were startlingly kind. Quite at random I recall the hospitality of Steve Stubert at Point Pelee, who helped build our camper! Al and Eurithe Purdy, who gave us sunctuary at Ameliasburgh, Père Raoul Gagnon, who included us as fellow celebrants at les Adorations nocturnes, at Notre Dame, in Place d'Armes, during long weeks of research in Montréal. And Elspeth and Peter Buitenhuis, who befriended us at the same period—we were staying at the Hotel Nelson, and Robert Lemieux, living across the hall, loaned us his records generously. Benoit Cote, welcoming us like long lost brothers, on the Ile d'Orleans. Larry Bache, whose apocalyptic generosity of person, at Mountain View, truly opened New Brunswick to us. Ken Windsor, professor in Fredericton, assuring us that our sense of correlation between the Christian doctrine of Real Presence and early Canadiana was not merely whacky! William Prouty, receiving us with Tio Pepe and Indian curry in old Loyalist Saint John (how to feel "At Home" for ever, in five minutes!). George MacLaren, in Halifax, quietly proving to me by his

very presence that Upper Canadians truly do have something to learn from the folk-genteel culture of the Maritimes.

And in Trout River, Newfoundland, where we finally settled for two weeks editing (and stayed six months!), the startling hospitality of Catherine and Jim Snook and the widespread Snookery; and of Mariam and Ches Barnes. Without their constant moose stews, rabbit pies, and partridge berry jam—combined with hours of family serenity, this book would have died an unnatural death.

Of course this book could not have been lived at all without the presence and persistance of John McConnell. Thanks to him, what started out as a "furniture safari" truly became what it should, a "safari of the soul."

Three friends made a combined gift of $10,000 so that—amidst poor circumstances—I could write this book at all. I long to share their names with you. But they will want to remain anonymous. For me, they are latter-day Medicis.

John de Visser is the visual voice of this book. In Canada, I see the new with old eyes. He sees the old with new eyes. Much of the celebration herein is his!

Scott Symons

Scott Symons

Scott Symons was born in 1933. As well as having been a journalist, professor, curator, and novelist, he has worked as a lumberjack on the West Coast; currently, he lives in Trout River, Newfoundland, and fishes for lobster.

Scott Symons has been called "a writer uniquely capable of seeing us through the history and artifacts of sensibility," and of his work it has been said that "a man has been relentlessly honest with himself in a way that is not at all typical." Personally, Symons says, "I am an unabashed revolutionary radical Tory!"

Scott Symons has published two novels with McClelland and Stewart: *Place d'Armes* and *Civic Square*.

John de Visser

John de Visser was born in 1930 "in a small town in rural Holland, not far from where both Pieter Breughal and Vincent van Gogh spent their youths."

His work has been called both brilliant and revealing, beautiful and powerful. A reviewer has said that "de Visser does not take photographs—he paints the elements of life with a camera." Another has said, "de Visser is that rare genius to whom the lens becomes an instrument of inner vision."

John de Visser collaborated with Farley Mowat to produce the McClelland and Stewart book on Newfoundland, "*This Rock within the Sea.*"

Heritage
A Romantic Look at Early Canadian Furniture

Design by David Shaw and Don Fernley

The typeface used in this book
is Cartier, designed by the late Carl Dair
and set on Linofilm by
Mono Lino Typesetting Company Ltd., Toronto.

Heritage was printed and bound in Italy by
Arnoldo Mondadori, Officine Grafiche,
Verona.

First edition, 1971